CAMBRIDGE MUSIC HANDBOOKS
Dvořák: Cello Concerto

Dvořák's Cello Concerto, composed during his second stay in America, is one of the most popular works in the orchestral repertoire. This guide explores Dvořák's reasons for composing a concerto for an instrument which he at one time considered unsuitable for solo work, its relationship to his American period compositions and how it forms something of a bridge with his operatic interests. A particular focus is the Concerto's unique qualities: why it stands apart in terms of form, melodic character and texture from the rest of Dvořák's orchestral music. The role of the dedicatee of the work, Hanuš Wihan, in its creation is also considered, as well as are performing traditions as they have developed in the twentieth century. In addition the guide explores the extraordinary emotional background to the work which links it intimately to the woman who was probably Dvořák's first love.

JAN SMACZNY is Hamilton Harty Professor of Music at the Queen's University of Belfast and has written widely on many aspects of Czech music.

CAMBRIDGE MUSIC HANDBOOKS

GENERAL EDITOR Julian Rushton

Dvořák: Cello Concerto

Jan Smaczny

CAMBRIDGE
UNIVERSITY PRESS

PUBLISHED BY THE PRESS SYNDICATE OF THE UNIVERSITY OF CAMBRIDGE
The Pitt Building, Trumpington Street, Cambridge, United Kingdom

CAMBRIDGE UNIVERSITY PRESS
The Edinburgh Building, Cambridge CB2 2RU, UK   http://www.cup.cam.ac.uk
40 West 20th Street, New York NY 10011-4211, USA   http://www.cup.org
10 Stamford Road, Oakleigh, Melbourne 3166, Australia

First published 1999

Printed in the United Kingdom at the University Press, Cambridge

Typeset in Ehrhardt MT 10½/13, in QuarkXPress™   [SE]

A catalogue record for this book is available from the British Library

Library of Congress cataloguing in publication data
Smaczny, Jan.
Dvořák cello concerto / Jan Smaczny.
p.   cm. – (Cambridge music handbooks)
Includes bibliographical references, discography, and index.
ISBN 0 521 66050 5 (hardback); 0 521 66903 0 (paperback)
1. Dvořák, Antonín, 1841–1904.   Concertos, violoncello, orchestra,
op. 104, B minor.   I. Title.   II. Series.
MT130.D9S6   1999
784.2'74–dc21   98-52746 CIP MN

ISBN 0 521 66050 5 hardback
ISBN 0 521 66903 0 paperback

For Duncan Fielden

Contents

Preface and acknowledgements

In an interview with John Tibbetts, the cellist Lynn Harrell spoke movingly about the emotional depth of Dvořák's Cello Concerto, adding that it was a 'unique piece of music'. Few would disagree, but in some ways the extreme popularity of the Concerto – at present over sixty recordings can be listed – has concealed its unusual qualities; while certainly not breeding contempt for the work, its familiarity might seem to obviate the need for close examination since its appeal is evident to any listener. And yet, the closer one looks, the more surprising this Concerto becomes. In form, texture and melodic style it stands apart from the totality of Dvořák's other orchestral works; fascinating too is the way in which the emotional content of the Concerto, felt by so many, can be linked to a personal epiphany with some degree of certainty. This book is offered in part as a guide to the uniqueness of the work, its rich emotional background, the role it filled in Dvořák's working life in America and as a link with the rest of his career.

Charting the history of this remarkable work – the fact that he composed a cello concerto at all is part of the surprise – turned into a process of revelation; a seemingly familiar friend became at times a near stranger and finally, once again, a friend, though certainly one who should not be taken for granted. As with all great works, however much is said about them, there will still remain a great many avenues to explore; certainly, one of the most encouraging aspects of having been so close to the Concerto is that throughout it retained its freshness and ability to surprise. With that thought in mind, I hope those reading the following study will see beyond its conclusions to a new starting point for enquiry.

Nearly everyone I have spoken to about Dvořák and his Cello Concerto in the last few years deserves a mention at the head of this volume; focusing on a single work inevitably leads to a certain monomania, so apologies as well as thanks to all those who have suffered from this particular interest. Where basic research on Dvořák is concerned, the mother-lode is to be found in Jarmil Burghauser's *Thematic Catalogue* and the complete edition of Dvořák's letters and documents, whose team of editors is triumphantly led by Milan Kuna; no thanks can be too great for access to these resources. In addition, the late Jarmil Burghauser must take a bow where nearly anything relating to Dvořák studies is concerned, not only for his own extensive work, but for his generosity in presenting me with so many ideas. In getting to grips with the manuscript material relating to the Concerto, Markéta Hallová was of inestimable help, not just in her capacity as director of the Dvořák Museum, but as an acute scholar of his work in her own right. Peter Alexander was hugely generous in providing copies of Kovařík's writings and insights in coming to terms with Dvořák's time in, and understanding of, America. Mike Beckerman, in between turning the ether blue with some of the most entertaining one-liners ever to be unleashed on e-mail, has been generous to a fault with both facts and ideas. An additional regiment has enriched my view of Dvořák's Concerto with its thoughts, chief among it are Jitka Slavíková, Alan Houtchens, Ron Speirs and Christopher Hogwood. For help and enthusiasm in examining the performance history of the Concerto and the work's technical peculiarities, I offer heartfelt thanks to Basil Deane. For library backup and support for travel in quest of the meaning of this glorious work, I am grateful to the University of Birmingham and the Queen's University of Belfast. Penny Souster at Cambridge University Press has been assiduous in pursuit of the finished article, for which I thank her, and Julian Rushton has throughout the creative process shown magisterial good sense, good taste and good humour. Finally, even apart from his astonishing technical expertise in turning my manuscript music examples into something a reader can profit from, I must thank Duncan Fielden for his forbearance in dealing so gently with an untidy and undisciplined author.

1

Dvořák and the cello

'As a solo instrument it isn't much good'

In one of the more substantial reminiscences of Dvořák by a pupil, Ludmila Vojáčková-Wechte retailed the composer's feelings regarding the cello:

> 'The cello', Dvořák said, 'is a beautiful instrument, but its place is in the orchestra and in chamber music. As a solo instrument it isn't much good. Its middle register is fine – that's true – but the upper voice squeaks and the lower growls. The finest solo-instrument, after all, is – and will remain – the violin. I have also written a 'cello-concerto, but am sorry to this day I did so, and I never intend to write another. I wouldn't have written that one had it not been for Professor Wihan. He kept buzzing it into me and reminding me of it, till it was done. I am sorry to this day for it!'[1]

Faced with this extraordinary revelation about Dvořák's attitude towards one of his greatest works, the astonished reader can at first only echo Ludmila Vojáčková-Wechte's interpretation of his comments: 'Maybe this opinion was meant more for the actual "squeaky and grumpy" instrument, than for the composition'.[2] Another possible reaction to his comments is that Dvořák was pulling the leg of a naïve composition pupil; the composer had a sarcastic streak which, as many of his wards found to their cost, he was more than happy to unleash on the unwary. But corroboration for his view that the cello was better suited to orchestral and chamber music (Dvořák admired in particular the use of the cellos in the Andante con moto of Beethoven's Fifth Symphony, presumably at the opening and from bar 49; on both occasions they are doubled by violas) comes from an account by another composition pupil, Josef Michl, who recounted that Dvořák considered the instrument 'rumbled' at both ends of the range.[3] Still more convincing evidence of

1

Dvořák's qualms about the cello as an effective concerto instrument is to be found in a letter he wrote from America to Alois Göbl on 10 December 1894 while hard at work on the Concerto – Göbl was a close musical friend in whom Dvořák often confided with directness and candour. Apart from enthusing about the virtues of revising compositions (Göbl had just attended, and enjoyed, Dvořák's radical revision of his opera *Dimitrij*), the unusual interest of the letter is the enthusiasm with which Dvořák talks about his new Concerto and of his own surprise at his enjoyment:

> And now to something more about music. I have actually finished the first movement of a Concerto for violoncello!! Don't be surprised about this, I too am amazed and surprised enough that I was so determined on such work.[4]

The remainder of the letter quotes the main themes of the first movement, notes that an ocean liner leaves for Europe and wishes his friend health and happiness in the New Year. Dvořák's words to Göbl communicate the delight of the converted and leave little doubt that he was astonished at his new-found interest in an instrument which hitherto he had regarded as an unlikely candidate for treatment in a concerto.

There is, however, a certain irony hovering over Dvořák's newly acquired enthusiasm of which Göbl, as a confidant of the composer, may have been aware. Dvořák's works for solo cello did not just comprise the Polonaise in A major (Polonéza, B 94), composed in 1879, and the handful of solo works he had written or arranged for performance with Hanuš Wihan in 1891; the skeleton in his closet was a Concerto for cello composed much earlier in his career.

Dvořák's first Cello Concerto

That Dvořák's pupils knew nothing of his first Cello Concerto (B 10) is not surprising. Few of his friends or contemporaries had much inkling of the true extent of the music he composed in his first decade of productivity (1860–70). Only the First String Quartet (B 8) and the Second Symphony (B 12) were performed in Dvořák's lifetime and none of the music was published;[5] moreover, much of it was lost or destroyed. Dvořák himself was extremely hazy about these works: he was certainly aware that his First

Symphony had been lost – apparently he sent the sole manuscript to a competition in Germany in 1865 and it was not returned.[6] Indeed, so hazy was Dvořák's recollection of many of these early works that several, including some whose manuscripts he still possessed, were entered into a list of 'compositions which I tore up and burned' made in 1887.[7] Interestingly, none of his seven lists of compositions, all of which include a range of early works,[8] mentions the Cello Concerto. Dvořák could be disingenuous about the compositional activities of the 1860s, the case of his first opera, *Alfred*, being a prime example: although he had the manuscript of the opera bound, he did not draw attention to *Alfred* in any interview about his early life or include it in any list of compositions. While Dvořák may have harboured a certain embarrassment that his first opera was composed to a German libretto,[9] there seems to be no obvious reason for reticence concerning his first Cello Concerto.

Dvořák completed this first Cello Concerto, in A major, in an unorchestrated piano score with a complete solo part on 30 June 1865, in between the composition of his first two symphonies. The work was dedicated to Ludevít Peer (1847–1904), a friend and colleague in the cello section of the Provisional Theatre's orchestra (Dvořák was a viola player in this tiny band from its foundation in November 1862 to the summer of 1871). Peer was a fine player who was already performing in the theatre orchestra while still only in his late teens and before he had graduated from the Conservatory; his leaving Prague at the end of the summer of 1865, taking the manuscript of the Concerto with him, may on the one hand have stopped the composer from orchestrating the work, but on the other it also prevented Dvořák from destroying it in one of his periodic conflagrations of early compositions.[10]

Along with the first two symphonies and much of Dvořák's early chamber music, the Cello Concerto was written on a large scale; in fact, had it had four movements rather than the customary three, it would have been longer than either symphony, each of which approaches an hour in playing time. In design, the Concerto is a good deal more experimental than the first two symphonies: all three movements are linked, the first two by a brief accompanied 'quasi recitativo' and the second and third by a long portentous bridge passage. Another feature which, in practice if not effect, looks forward to Dvořák's second Cello Concerto is the recall of material from the introduction to the first movement in the finale's coda. The use of material from the first movement as a kind of clinching gesture in finales was, of course, relatively common at the time, and was to become a major feature in the works of Dvořák's maturity; though the early Cello Concerto is an interesting example of this practice, Dvořák had already tried it in his First String Quartet.

The unorchestrated and unrevised form in which the Concerto survives makes judgement about the composer's final intention for the work difficult. Its huge dimensions may well have encouraged wholesale cutting, as in his revision of the First String Quartet before a performance in 1888; if so, Dvořák might well have turned his attention to the solo cello part: after the lengthy introduction, lasting 136 bars, the cello part only rests once in the first movement and plays continuously in the slow movement; the first substantial break for the soloist comes at the start of the rondo. The relentless nature of the cello part – which, apart from its size, almost always has the soloist in the limelight (often doubling the main melodic line in the 'orchestra') and only rarely takes an accompanimental role – may have reflected the composer's admiration for the energy and vitality of Peer, who was certainly an animated player; it is, however, impossible to escape the thought that Dvořák, had he had the opportunity to orchestrate the work, would have revised the solo part down to a more manageable length and provided a more sensible balance between frontline solo work and accompaniment.

As a competent viola player,[11] Dvořák had more than an elementary grasp of string technique, and there is evident intelligence in the placing of lyrical lines suitably high in the instrument's register. But his approach to other aspects of cello technique is limited: he did not, for example, make any effort to explore the possibilities of multiple stopping, a feature which is such an impressive aspect of the rhetorical language of the second Concerto. Occasionally in the early Concerto Dvořák shows himself adept at extending phrases with mellifluous figuration, just as he was to do again in the B minor Cello Concerto, but rarely does he achieve the subtle integration that makes the later work so satisfying. A comparison between the sequential extensions to the second subjects of the first movement of the A major Cello Concerto and the finale of the B minor Cello Concerto illustrates the point: in the latter, the material for the sequence is clearly derived from figuration in the second full beat of the theme (see Ex. 1.1b, figure y); in the earlier

Ex. 1.1(a) and (b)

Concerto the sequential material (see Ex. 1.1a, figure *x*) is an attractive afterthought rather than a true development. Other aspects of figuration are shared between the two works, notably the ornamental articulation of arpeggio figures: rising in the example from the first movement of the A major Concerto (Ex. 1.2a, figure *x*) and falling in the first movement of the B minor Concerto (Ex. 1.2b, figure *y*).

Ex. 1.2(a) and (b)

Parallels such as these are as much the result of natural instinct – Dvořák always had a tendency to elaborate basic outlines, often to avoid an exact repetition – as the exercise of memory. Broader structural features and aspects of tone, however, may have lodged in Dvořák's mind more readily than figurational details. Neither Concerto has an extended formal cadenza, and there is little in the way of combative virtuosity or conflict between soloist and orchestra in either work. The return of material from the first movement in the last has already been mentioned, but the first movements of the two Concertos have in common a more unusual structural feature: their recapitulations begin with the second subject, a practice confined in Dvořák's output to these two Concertos. In both works, the need to short-circuit the recapitulation may well have been prompted by the presence of a large-scale opening ritornello. But if Dvořák was remembering his lost early Concerto when penning the same point in his later work, he avoided any similarity in manner: the recapitulation of the first movement of the A major Concerto is a muted if attractive affair in which the dynamic markings are *dolce pp*; in the B minor Concerto the recapitulation is a highpoint underlined by the use of the full orchestra and marked *ff*.

A final point of contact between the two Concertos also occurs in the first movement. In tone and, to an extent, outline, there is considerable correlation between the first and second subjects of these two Cello Concertos – certainly more than in the comparable thematic

Ex. 1.3(a) and (b)

elements in Dvořák's Violin and Piano Concertos. The most obvious resemblance is in the presentation of the first themes (cf. Exx. 1.3a and 1.3b), both of which are strikingly rhetorical with balanced rising and falling phrases for the soloist. Comparison can also be made between the second themes, both of which have a distinctly vocal quality (cf. Ex. 1.1a and Ex. 4.2b). The second subject of the A major Cello Concerto's first movement was borrowed from the main Allegro of the First String Quartet, also in A major, where it is set in a jaunty $\frac{6}{8}$ time; in its more easeful, common-time guise in the Cello Concerto its full-throated lyricism undoubtedly looks forward to Dvořák's mature melodic style.

'Its place is in . . . chamber music'

Dvořák's view that the cello as soloist was best suited to chamber music is somewhat paradoxical: if the timbral qualities of the instrument were unsuitable for solo work in a concerto, why should it fare better when taking a solo line in a chamber work? Dvořák's use of the cello in a chamber context is in fact extensive and imaginative, although it is also relatively specialised. Among the works written in the same decade as the A major Concerto there is little to suggest more than a routine interest in the instrument for chamber purposes. Although the cello is far from neglected in Dvořák's first two surviving chamber compositions, the A minor String Quintet (B 7) and the A major String Quartet, there are no notable solos. Some six years after composing the A major Cello Concerto, Dvořák wrote a sonata for the instrument; completed on 4 January

1871, it is known only from an incipit (which indicates that it was in F minor), and an analysis by Otakar Šourek.[12] From this we can deduce that the sonata, in common with the astonishing E minor Quartet (B 19) which precedes it in the thematic catalogue, is marked by a fascination with thematic integration and a boldly experimental approach to tonality. Unfortunately, although Šourek must have had the cello part from which to make his deductions, this no longer appears to exist.[13]

Although there is an expressive cello solo line in the Andante introduction to the early B-flat major String Quartet (B 17, ?1868–70), this is something of an exception. Dvořák begins to take more interest in the cello's solo role in chamber music in his works where the string parts are joined by the piano, or in compositions – such as the String Quintet with double bass in G major (op. 77, B 49) and the String Sextet in A-flat major (op. 48, B 80) – in which the presence of another bass instrument allows the cello more liberty. In his first surviving work for piano and strings, the First Piano Quintet (A major, op. 5, B 28) of 1872, the cello part is marked 'solo'; it is the first instrument to be heard after the piano introduction, a feature shared by Dvořák's much more celebrated A major Piano Quintet (op. 81, B 155) composed some sixteen years later. In the slow movement of the earlier quintet the cello often takes an expressive lead and in the finale it introduces the main second subject. There are similar solo opportunities for the cello in the slow movements of the B-flat major (op. 21, B 51) and G minor Piano Trios (op. 26, B 56) of 1875 and 1876, where the instrument is used in its tenor register and marked *espressivo*, and in the First Piano Quartet (D major, op. 23, B 53), where it initiates most of the significant material in the first and last movements.

As Dvořák's style matured during the 1880s, there is little sign of any revulsion or embarrassment attached to the use of the cello in chamber music: the cello has significant solo opportunities in the slow movements of the F minor Piano Trio (op. 65, B 130) and the Second Piano Quartet (op. 87, B 162), and its role at the start of the Second Piano Quintet is well known, though on balance in this work Dvořák shows slightly more preference for his own instrument, the viola. The one composition of the keyboard accompanied variety in which the cello does not take such a prominent role is his Bagatelles (op. 47, B 79), for two violins, cello and harmonium; the trio sonata instrumentation necessitates a somewhat different disposition of forces, with the cello articulating and energising the bass.

Dvořák's surviving solo works for cello and piano are something of a miscellany. The Polonaise, composed for a concert in Turnov on 29 June 1879 and first performed by the cellist Alois Neruda (1837–99), is an attractive blend of lyricism and virtuosity. The fact that Dvořák did not give the work an opus number nor attempted to have it published – unlike the other items in the concert, including the Bagatelles and the Mazurek for violin and piano (op. 49, B 89) – should not be read as a negative judgement: it seems the piece went missing shortly after the concert. The work, however, survived in a copy which Neruda gave to the young cellist Wilhelm Jeral, who eventually published it in 1925 (Dvořák may have been cutting his losses when he used a secondary melody and the theme of the central section of the work for the scherzo and finale respectively of his String Quartet in C major (op. 61, B 121) composed two years later).

If it had been to hand, Dvořák would doubtless have made use of the Polonaise when casting around for solo items for an extensive concert tour of Bohemia and Moravia made from early January to the end of March 1892 (arranged by the Prague publisher Velebín Urbánek and intended as a kind of farewell to his fellow Czechs and the concert societies he had visited in the previous fifteen years). The centrepiece of the tour was a set of six Dumky for Piano Trio (known nowadays as the Piano Trio in E minor, op. 90, B 166, 'Dumky'). Although the Dumky were rich in solo opportunities for the cello, Dvořák needed some makeweights to play with his violinist, Ferdinand Lachner, and the cellist Hanuš Wihan. Lachner performed the Mazurek and the piano and violin version of the Romantic Pieces (Romantické kusy, op. 75, B 150), but, in the absence of the Polonaise, there was nothing for Wihan. Dvořák filled the gap in a matter of three days (beginning on Christmas Day 1891) with the Rondo in G minor (op. 94, B 171), an arrangement of two of the first set of Slavonic Dances (nos. 8 and 3, B 172) and another arrangement, *Silent Woods* (*Klid*, B 173) from the piano duet cycle *From the Bohemian Forest* (*Ze Šumavy*, op. 68, B 133). All four works show Dvořák very much at home with the cello as soloist. The tessitura is high, with Dvořák exploiting the singing qualities of the instrument; he also shows a fondness for focusing on Wihan's capacity for high-pitched trills in the Rondo (the Rondo and *Silent Woods* are discussed in the next chapter, where the role of the orchestral versions of these works is considered). As Dvořák played the accompaniment to these pieces while he toured nearly forty towns in Bohemia and Moravia, the potential for more extended treatment of the cello as a solo instrument cannot have been lost on him.

2

Preludes to the Concerto

Cello and orchestra together for the first time

If Dvořák's objections to the cello were largely based on timbral considerations, as his pupils' testimony suggests, his experience on tour with Wihan would have done much to allay his fears. During his stay in America, and even before he considered beginning work on a concerto, his mind was turning once again towards the cello as a solo instrument, though doubts as to the viability of the cello when pitted against an orchestra seem to have remained. These surfaced while orchestrating the Rondo and *Silent Woods* in New York in October 1893. Along with revisions to his Ninth Symphony ('From the New World', op. 95, B 178), these two orchestrations comprised Dvořák's first creative work on his return to New York after an extended summer holiday in the Czech community of Spillville in Iowa. Exactly why he made the arrangements is not known, but they may have been prompted by his German publisher Simrock, with whom he was re-establishing good relations. (The two men had fallen out badly over Simrock's unwillingness to publish Dvořák's Eighth Symphony in 1890 and professional relations were effectively suspended until the summer of 1893.) Dvořák wrote to Simrock early in July offering, in a package that included the Ninth Symphony and the 'American' Quartet, the Rondo for cello at the relatively modest price of 500 marks.[1] Simrock at this point might well have suggested orchestral versions, since he published them along with the piano originals the following year. For his part, Dvořák saw it as an opportunity to claim an extra 1,000 mark fee for the two arrangements and the piano duet version of the 'Dumky' Trio.[2]

Dvořák's approach to instrumentation in these arrangements is best described as gingerly. The orchestral forces in both were unusually

11

Ex. 2.1

modest given his normal practice at the time: for *Silent Woods* the orchestra comprised one flute, two clarinets, two bassoons, one horn and strings. Throughout both works, Dvořák was at pains to prevent the cello from being swamped. His task was easier in *Silent Woods*, in which the dynamic hardly rises above *piano* except at occasional points of emphasis. While in general the orchestral palette lacks the inspired colouring of the B minor Cello Concerto, Dvořák at one point anticipates the kind of small-scale chamber combination that becomes such a notable feature of the orchestration in the slow movement of the Cello Concerto. An arabesque figure from the right hand of the piano original is given to the flute while the cello solo provides bass movement (see Ex. 2.1); although it lacks the rapturous quality of the cello's duet with the solo flute in the slow movement of the Concerto, it is clear that Dvořák was beginning to think along the lines of effective orchestral combinations with the cello (cf. Ex. 2.1 with Ex. 6.2).

The instrumentation in the Rondo is also modest, though slightly different from *Silent Woods*, comprising two oboes, two bassoons, strings and, significantly, timpani. Although the Rondo has nothing like the emotional scope of the finale of the Cello Concerto, which is also a rondo, the proximity of composition prompts comparison. There are superficial similarities, notably the hectoring orchestral unison built into the first presentation of the rondo theme and certain aspects of cello figuration. Of more significance is the use to which the timpani are put in quietly underpinning the cello line in the return of the Rondo theme after the first episode, and their presence just before the second appearance of the subsidiary material, moments Dvořák may well have remembered when penning the final descent of the cello in the coda of the finale of the Concerto. Apart from these specific instances, the orchestration is attractive, if somewhat inhibited by comparison with the Concerto: the pairs of wind instruments in both arrangements tend to supply a chordal glow articulated by more mobile string figuration; certainly there is nothing of the sinuous intertwining between woodwind and soloist that is such a memorable aspect of instrumentation in the Concerto.

'A sonata for cello'

While Dvořák clearly continued to harbour doubts about the possibilities of combining the cello with the full resources of the normal symphony orchestra, thoughts of other solo works for cello surfaced more than once during 1893. While sketching his Sonatina in G major (op. 100, B 183) for violin and piano, dedicated to all six of his children as a celebration of his hundredth opus,[3] he also jotted down an idea for a cello sonata, perhaps as a companion piece. This passing thought amounted to almost nothing, but somewhat earlier in the year he had assayed some more substantial sketches for a Sonata for Cello and Piano ('Sonata Celo a Piano'[4]), probably made in June or July.[5]

The sketches comprise three separate thematic ideas: the beautiful initial melody has become well known as the theme associated with Rusalka in the opera of the same name (op. 114, B 203) written seven years later; the second was used for the opening idea of the Allegro vivo second movement scherzo of the E flat major String Quintet (op. 97, B 180). No attention has been given to the theme on the verso of page 17: written on two staves, the lower part seems to be forming a rudimentary accompaniment to the cello part which enters in the third bar (see Ex. 2.2a). The accompaniment turns into a somewhat obsessive ostinato (not an unusual feature of some of Dvořák's American sketches), but in rhythm and intervallic direction, the first bar is remarkably similar to the

Ex. 2.2(a) and (b)

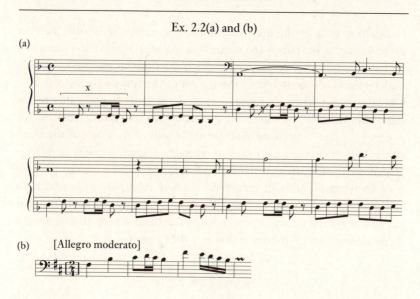

terse opening of the rondo theme of the Cello Concerto (cf. Ex. 2.2a and Ex. 2.2b); it also shares the key in which Dvořák began the continuous sketch of the Concerto: D minor. In an extensive commentary on the continuous sketch, John Clapham makes no reference to this early appearance of an idea used in the Concerto, probably because the sketches for the Concerto appear to be largely hermetic.[6]

The resemblance suggests that Dvořák was still using material from his early 'American' phase even when working on a composition which is often regarded as something of a departure from his American manner (see Chapter 3). But equally important is the fact that Dvořák was still toying with an idea for a solo work for the cello; the sound was in his mind even if a firm intention to compose something extended for the instrument had yet to materialise. A crucial experience was all that was needed to push him towards a much fuller realisation of these intentions.

'The Road to Damascus': Dvořák and Victor Herbert's Second Cello Concerto

According to Ludmila Vojáčková-Wechte, Wihan had pressed Dvořák to write a concerto for the cello. Dvořák's serious misgivings about the viability of such a work would have been fuelled by the lack of an extensive contemporary repertoire for the instrument. Against this background, the arrival on the scene of a new work for cello and orchestra would likely have been of intense interest to him. Such an opportunity was provided by the première of Victor Herbert's Second Cello Concerto on 10 March 1894:[7] the composer played the solo part and the orchestra was conducted by Dvořák's friend, the conductor Anton Seidl.

Herbert (1859–1924) was an Irish-born cellist and composer whose family settled in Germany when he was only seven years old. Studying with Bernhard Cossmann and Max Seifriz in Stuttgart, his training as a cellist was entirely German in nature. Early successes followed, and Herbert was in demand as a soloist and chamber music performer throughout Europe. In 1886 he married the opera singer Therese Foerster, and in October of the same year they moved to the USA where they were both engaged by the Metropolitan Opera. To enhance his income in New York, Herbert joined the teaching staff of Jeanette M. Thurber's National Conservatory of Music in 1889, and was head of the cello class when Dvořák took up the directorship of the National Conservatory on 1 October 1892. His relationship with Dvořák was good, and in a letter to the German critic Hans Schnoor in 1922, he painted a warmly affectionate portrait of the composer,[8] stating fulsomely that: 'We all loved him, for he was so kind and affable – his great big beautiful eyes radiated warmth – and of such childlike simplicity and naturalness – and when he left us, we lost not only a master-musician whose presence had had a marked influence on musical activities in N.Y. [New York] but a most admirable, lovable friend'.

In the same letter, Herbert mentioned Dvořák's presence at the première of his Second Cello Concerto saying: 'Dr Dvořák came back to the "Stimm-Zimmer" – threw his arms around me, saying before many members of the orchestra: famos! famos! – ganz famos!'[9] The impact of the concerto on Dvořák, a fact accepted by commentators from Šourek to Clapham, was reported mainly by his amanuensis in New York, Joseph Jan Kovařík.[10] The third of Kovařík's articles about the composer,[11] describing Dvořák's concert-going activities, includes an account of Dvořák's reaction to Herbert's Concerto which is worth quoting at length:

If I am not mistaken, it was during Dvořák's second stay in New York that Victor Herbert played his own 'Cello Concerto with the Philharmonic. Dvořák, who admired Herbert as a 'cellist, was very anxious to hear the work. We attended the Friday afternoon's public rehearsal, as the doctor rarely cared to go out evenings. After Mr. Herbert got through the concerto, all that Dvořák said was 'that fellow played wonderfully' – his exact words. Nothing more was said of the playing or the composition.

Just about dinner time the next day, Dr. Dvořák, without any preliminary remarks, said: 'There is one wonderfully clever spot in that 'Cello Concerto that I must hear again', and, the dinner over, we wended our way toward Carnegie Hall to listen to the same programme.

Before the 'Cello Concerto, Dvořák said: 'Now, when I give you a slight push, then listen carefully, as I want you to tell me why I regard that particular part as being so clever.'

'Oh, very well, I'll listen', I said.

The concerto started, and was going along very nicely when suddenly I received a jolt which nearly knocked me out of my seat, and the next moment I was busy rubbing my arm on the spot where the Doctor's elbow landed.

The concerto over, Dvořák asked how I liked the 'clever spot'. I said I did not hear it.

'Well, why didn't you listen? I gave you the "push" as I said I would, didn't I?' asked Dvořák.

'Yes, you surely did, Doctor. I got the "push" all right, but when I got it I had something more important to do than to listen'.

'Well, it's too bad you didn't hear what wonderful use he (referring to Mr. Herbert) has made of the trombones without overpowering the solo instrument in the least'.

A couple of days later, Dvořák borrowed the score of the concerto – then in manuscript – and looked it over with much satisfaction.

'Wonderful!' was all he said.

Kovařík's account smacks a little of the awe-struck admirer recounting an event in almost parable-like terms, but Dvořák was a creature of habit and interrupting an evening at home with the family certainly suggests something of moment had occurred. There is more than a ring of truth about Dvořák's reaction to Herbert's handling of the orchestra in relation to the solo cello. If his avoidance of brass instruments in the arrangements of the Rondo and *Silent Woods* is some indication of his doubts about the viability of the cello in a full orchestral context, it seems more

solo horn plays a reminiscence of the opening theme of the first movement (see Ex. 6.13b). Other than this, Dvořák's lesson in handling the orchestra is more one of general principle than particular effect. (Herbert's energising of accompanying string lines by means of reiterated semiquavers is a familiar technique from the Classical era onwards and was certainly well known to Dvořák, as his own Violin Concerto written fifteen years earlier shows.) There is, for example, none of the exquisite, almost chamber-like, combinations in Herbert's work that Dvořák adopts so successfully in all three movements of his Concerto; nor did Dvořák take anything from Herbert's musical language, which leans heavily in this work on Liszt and Tchaikovsky. Herbert's formal scheme looks back to Saint-Saëns' A minor Cello Concerto (op. 33): the movements run into one another and in the finale Herbert reworks material from the first movement; there is also a prominent place for the main melody of the slow movement. While Dvořák quoted from the first two movements of his Concerto in the finale, these are intended as significant reminiscences rather than as attempts to develop the material further.

Certain aspects of the rhetoric in Herbert's Concerto also seem to have struck Dvořák: he may, for example, have decided against a cadenza following Herbert's lead – a judgement he defended vigorously in the face of Wihan's desire for one in the finale; against the background of a pervasively full orchestral texture in both Concertos, a limited amount of expressive, loosely measured solo writing is desirable, but a full-blown cadenza would be entirely out of place. Another point where comparison between the two works is fruitful is at moments of recapitulation: in the case of Herbert's Concerto, the finale, and in Dvořák's, the first movement. Leaving aside the widely differing characters of the two movements, there are, nevertheless, strong similarities in outline at these points as well as in the treatment of the solo line and orchestra. In both, after a passage of relative stillness in the development, the temperature rises, with a crescendo in the orchestra supported by gradually more intense virtuosity in the solo line. A climactic chord and solo descent (in Dvořák it is down a dominant seventh arpeggio) are followed by a dramatic chromatic ascent into the recapitulation (cf. Exx. 2.4a and 2.4b). The actual points of recapitulation are characterised very differently: famously, Dvořák begins his recapitulation with his second subject,

Ex. 2.4(a) and (b)

while Herbert combines his main idea with the theme of the slow movement played by the solo cello. The resemblance between the two passages, however, is striking less for any melodic similarity than for the dynamic outline and the bold rhetoric of the cello's sweeping lead back. Features such as these do not, *in toto*, add up to a major debt to Herbert; though not impervious to another composer's influence in his maturity, there is no sign that Dvořák was moved to emulate any aspect of Herbert's musical language. But the role of Herbert's Concerto as exemplar and ultimately progenitor cannot be ignored or belittled; without Herbert's pioneering work it seems doubtful that Dvořák would have composed the concerto requested by Wihan.

3

The Concerto and Dvořák's 'American manner'

The stylistic developments which occurred in Dvořák's music during the preparations for his visit to the United States and, in particular, during the first year and a half of his stay there are striking. Though different in many aspects of detail, these changes mirror the shift of emphasis seen in his work in the early to mid-1870s when, in a matter of three years, he moved away from the highly experimental compositional stance he had adopted towards the end of the 1860s towards the more moderate and approachable manner that characterised the music which brought him national and international fame in the 1880s.

The phenomenal success of Dvořák's 'American' works certainly requires consideration, as does the generally held view that the Cello Concerto, although conceived and composed in America, marks a significant retreat from the stylistic features he adopted in the New World.[1] It would be a mistake, however, to assume that Dvořák's 'American' style erupted on his arrival in New York. Before he set off for the United States on 15 September 1892 Dvořák had already prepared a work for his inaugural concert. This was not the cantata *The American Flag* suggested by his American patroness, Mrs Jeanette M. Thurber, but the *Te Deum* (op. 103, B 176). Mrs Thurber was not only set on Dvořák providing a work that was suitable as the composer's introduction to New York, but also one that was appropriate to the Columbus celebrations of 1892. Luckily, she was somewhat tardy in finding a text, and by the end of June when she sent Joseph Rodman Drake's wretched poem 'The American Flag', Dvořák was already at work on the sketch of a *Te Deum*, one of her suggested alternatives.

The *Te Deum* already shows the wealth of pentatonic figures, driving ostinati, direct utterance and pastoral tone which are often cited as key constituents of Dvořák's American manner.[2] Many of these features were present, of course, in his earlier work; a tendency towards pentatonic colouring in melody and figuration dates back to Dvořák's First String Quartet of 1862 and appears on numerous later occasions, notably in the Fifth and Eighth Symphonies.[3] There is perhaps a greater use of it in the works which were composed on the approach to the visit to America, in particular the Second Piano Quintet (op. 87, B 155), the Requiem (op. 89, B 165), the 'Dumky' Trio (op. 90, B 166), and the overtures *In Nature's Realm* (*V přírodě*, op. 91, B 168) and *Carnival* (*Karneval*, op. 92, B 169). Alongside this development in melodic language was a move away from what is usually construed as a phase of Viennese Classical Romanticism, which had occupied him from the early to mid-1880s. To an extent this view is naïve, given the alternative strands of Dvořák's composing career, such as opera and oratorio, but it has a certain validity when abstract forms such as symphony and chamber music are considered. The Eighth Symphony, completed in 1889, marks a major break with the norms of intensive developmental writing associated with the Sixth and Seventh Symphonies. In chamber music, the Second Piano Quintet of 1887 fulfilled a similar role, especially when compared to the Piano Trio in F minor composed four years before; the finale of the Quintet is particularly notable not just for its extensive pentatonic figuration, but for the insistent repetition of certain ideas that anticipates Dvořák's practice in a number of the 'New World' works.

In America Dvořák adopted a marked simplicity of melodic outline, with ideas often seeming to exist quite separately from their surroundings; while certainly memorable, the themes in many of the American works do not have the plasticity that featured so strongly in Dvořák's music in the 1880s. The developmental potential in many of the movements composed in America is often vested in the short rhythmic ideas which are a subsidiary feature of the main melody and which lend themselves to assertive repetition and the building of sequence, as in the first movements of the 'New World' Symphony and the 'American' Quartet.

The new simplicity of melodic construction in these early American works also extended to formal outline. After the free-wheeling experiment of the Eighth Symphony in particular, the return to a near textbook presentation of sonata form in the first movements of the 'New World' Symphony and the 'American' Quartet is striking, and must in part reflect the composer's new approach to melodic content. But another factor was almost certainly in play.

When Jeannette Thurber opened her National Conservatory of Music in the autumn of 1885, with backing from her husband's wholesale food company and donations from a number of rich philanthropists, including Andrew Carnegie and William K. Vanderbilt, her aim was to provide a systematic training for musicians of talent along the lines of the Paris Conservatoire, where she had studied as a teenager. Possessed of formidable energy, Mrs Thurber persuaded the members of the United States Senate in 1891, for the first time in their history where such an organisation was concerned, to pass a Bill of Incorporation for the National Conservatory.[4] Close to her heart was the desire to attract a figure of international standing to lead her organisation, a feat she achieved in the same year as the Bill of Incorporation: 'In the year 1891 I was so fortunate as to secure Bohemia's foremost composer, Antonín Dvořák, as artistic director of the National Conservatory'. The impact of Dvořák's presence was immediate and far reaching, as Mrs Thurber gushed in her account of his stay: 'From the start he devoted himself to his new duties with the utmost zeal . . . . Many of our most gifted young men eagerly seized the opportunity of studying with him. Among these students were Harvey Worthington Loomis, Rubin Goldmark, Harry Rowe Shelley, William Arms Fisher, Harry T. Burleigh and Will Marion Cook, who now rank with our best composers.'[5]

Dvořák's pattern of teaching and the various statements made on the nature of his role in America suggest that he took his educative role very seriously.[6] Two letters from his pupils Rubin Goldmark and Michael Banner, sent respectively on 10 December 1893 and 29 July 1894, are eloquent evidence of their gratitude for Dvořák's efforts as a teacher.[7] The suggestion that during this early phase in New York Dvořák's pupils were very much part of a project to establish a national style of American music is confirmed by comments published in the *Chicago Tribune* of 13 August 1893 concerning the 'American colour' to be found in his String Quintet (op. 97, B 180) and the 'New World' Symphony;[8] in the same article he spoke with approval of his 'most promising and gifted' pupil Maurice Arnold Strathotte, whose 'Creole Dances' contained material 'in a style that accords with my ideas'. The presence of Strathotte, and another pupil, Loomis, at the première of the 'New World' Symphony, on 16 December 1893, also suggests a didactic dimension to the work – a means of harnessing colourful thematic material to clear formal outline as a suitable model for a generation of aspiring American composers.

While the actual impact of the Symphony on American composers will remain the subject of study and controversy,[9] there can be no doubting a strong localised effect and a clear perception of its novelty, as a letter to Dvořák from E. Francis Hyde, President of the Board of Directors of the Philharmonic Society of New York, indicates:

> The performance of this work at the Society's concerts of December 15th and 16th was epochal in its character, for it was the first production of a new work, by one of the greatest composers, written in America, embodying the sentiment and romance derived from a residence in America and a study of its native tone-expressions.
>
> The immediate and immense success of the work ... was a sincere gratification to the Society and testified not only to the greatness of the work, but also to the recognition by the audience of the Society of the justness of the title of your new tone-poem.[10]

While the didactic impulse may go some way to explaining the change in style apparent in these works, the liberating effect that New York and the United States in general had on Dvořák should not be discounted. In a long article entitled 'Music in America', Dvořák wrote with some force about certain qualities of the American character; although his prose was undoubtedly given a burnished rhetorical ring (unfamiliar from his writing in any language) by his collaborator Edwin Emerson Jr., the general thrust is clear:

> The two American traits which most impress the foreign observer, I find, are the unbounded patriotism and capacity for enthusiasm of most Americans. Unlike the more diffident inhabitants of other countries, who do not 'wear their hearts upon their sleeves', the citizens of America are always patriotic, and no occasion seems to be too serious or too slight for them to give expression to this feeling. Thus nothing better pleases the average American, especially the American youth, than to be able to say that this or that building, this or that new patent appliance, is the finest or the grandest in the world. This, of course, is due to that other trait – enthusiasm. The enthusiasm of most Americans for all things new is apparently without limit. It is the essence of what is called 'push' – American push. Every day I meet with this quality in my pupils. They are unwilling to stop at anything. In the matters relating to their art they are inquisitive to a degree that they want to go to the bottom of all things at once.[11]

Coupled to Dvořák's admiration for American enthusiasm was a fascination with the American respect for free thought and divergent ideas. In
an account of Anton Seidl, conductor of the Metropolitan Opera and the
New York Philharmonic Society, Dvořák waxed lyrical about liberal
American attitudes: 'He was a wild rebel and atheist, and often would say
terrible things. If people were to utter the things he said (in the Old
World) they would never get out of prison. But in America nobody takes
any notice.'[12] Dvořák's response to these attributes seems to have
resulted in an element of 'playing to the crowd' in many of the 'American' works, heard at its most obvious in the frank razzmatazz of the
closing bars of *The American Flag* and the 'New World' Symphony.
(That he had a clear notion of the 'popular' manner is evident from a
letter to his friend Alois Göbl, when he spoke about his Dumky for Piano
Trio as being of a popular character suitable for 'high and low'.[13])
Dvořák himself was almost gleefully aware of the developments in his
style in America. While at work on the 'New World' Symphony he wrote
to his friend Emil Kozánek about the fundamental difference between
the new symphony and his earlier ones: 'In short, anybody who has a
"nose" must sense the influence of America' – a sentiment he repeated in
similar terms only two days later to another Czech friend, Antonín
Rus.[14] The ready and open response, and the general lack of censure
which Dvořák encountered in America, may well have been another
strong contributory factor to a change in style; remote from the immediate scrutiny of the likes of Hanslick, he could branch away from the
Viennese Classicism that he had cultivated to an extent in the 1880s and
show a side of himself that was more open-hearted and, in a less self-con-
sciously cultivated society, more approachable.

The perceptible novelty of this manner and the fact that the Cello
Concerto seems to be something of a reversion to Dvořák's pre-American style are qualities noted by most commentators. For example,
Clapham, taking a lead from Šourek, states the now generally held view
when introducing the Cello Concerto in his 1966 study of Dvořák's life
and works: 'From its content it is clear that his thoughts were turning
homewards, and for the first time in an important work composed in
America we find the American colouring reduced to a bare
minimum'.[15] Some support for this view might seem to come from
Kovařík. During Dvořák's time in New York his unique status made

him a focus of interest concerning the very nature of American music. In a series of interviews and articles, among other things, he advanced theories about the viability of an American school of composition: 'In the Negro melodies of America I discover all that is needed for a great and noble school of music'.[16] Dvořák also spoke about the 'American colouring' he had endeavoured to incorporate in the works which he wrote in his first year in America: 'I have just completed a quintet for string instruments. . . . In this work I think there will be found the American colour with which I have endeavoured to infuse it. My new symphony [no. 9, *From the New World*] is also on the same lines, namely an endeavour to portray characteristics, such as are distinctly American'.[17] The enthusiasm and enthusiastic debate which greeted the first performance of the 'New World' Symphony clearly appalled Dvořák, who had something of a horror of controversy. According to Kovařík, some months after the première of the symphony Dvořák reacted badly to the suggestion that he was now an American composer: 'I was, I am, and I remain a Czech composer. I have only showed them the path they might take – how they should work. But I'm through with that! From this day forward I will write the way I wrote before.'[18] As with other quotes from the composer reported by Kovařík, the statement has a suspiciously neat and epigrammatic air, but the import is clear: not only were his early American works didactic in intent, but he was making a conscious decision to abandon the style. A number of the compositions written from the spring of 1894 onwards have been adduced as evidence of this apparent recidivism; after the *Biblical Songs* (op. 99, B 185), which were completed on 26 March 1894, these include the extensive revision of the grand opera *Dimitrij* (B 186), the *Humoresques* for piano solo (op. 101, B 187), the *Lullaby* (*Ukolébavka*) and *Capriccio* for piano (B 188), the two String Quartets in A-flat major and G major (opp. 105 and 106, B 192 and B 193) as well as the Cello Concerto.

The Cello Concerto exhibits a number of differences in approach to that adopted in the 'New World' Symphony, the 'American' Quartet and E flat major String Quintet, not least a much less orthodox attitude to form and thematic process in the first movement; there is also no longer a tendency to focus on small rhythmic fragments as the chief engines of transition and development. But if certain stylistic features in the Cello

25

Ex. 3.1

Ex. 3.2

Concerto separate it from the products of Dvořák's first fifteen months in America, there are also some marked similarities, particularly in aspects of thematic design. While Clapham notes the flattened seventh in the second bar of the opening theme, he is inclined to link it to the similarly modal opening of the Seventh Symphony, rather than to any American influence.[19] And yet, apart from obvious rhythmic differences, its melodic outline is almost identical to the opening theme of the finale of the 'New World' Symphony (see Ex 3.1; to facilitate comparison, the Cello Concerto melody is transposed from its original B minor into E minor). A number of more motivic features which can conveniently be described as 'American' also occur, for instance at the Tempo 1 marking at bar 110 in the first movement, where the cello solo provides a figurational development of the opening theme following a generally pentatonic shape (see Ex. 3.2). Much the same is true of the conclusion of the slow movement, with the solo cello's gentle pentatonic descent over a

26

Ex. 3.3

sustained G major chord in the strings and yearning, falling phrases in the flute and oboe (bars 162–3).

Beyond melodic and motivic considerations there is also the question of atmosphere; Beckerman's statement that 'this [American] period is dominated by pastoral tone'[20] is supported by a gathering of examples including the slow movements of the 'New World' Symphony and the Cello Concerto. No-one could miss the similarity between the efflorescent woodwind writing that precedes the main climax in the slow movement of the 'New World' Symphony (bars 90–3) and the rapturous response of the clarinet, flute and bassoon to the *quasi Cadenza* for the cello in the slow movement of the Cello Concerto (see bars 107–20); both passages are near-classic examples of the 'pastoral tone' to which Beckerman refers.

The much celebrated second theme of the first movement of the Cello Concerto, for Tovey 'one of the most beautiful passages ever written for the horn',[21] poses a slightly different problem: at first sight, with its near-pentatonic design, it seems to share affinities with Dvořák's more recent American compositions. On his own admission, Dvořák had taken great trouble over this theme.[22] But its outline, especially that of the first phrase, is also nearly identical to the B major romance for Slavoj in act I of Dvořák's grand opera *Vanda*, composed in 1875, nearly twenty years before the Concerto (see Ex 3.3; to facilitate the comparison, the romance from *Vanda* has been transposed from its original B major into D major).

The question whether the Cello Concerto is more or less 'American' than other works written earlier in his stay is not really the issue; what is at issue is what we mean by Dvořák's 'American' style. As we have seen, it is possible to argue that some melodic elements are proximate to the 'New World' Symphony but also that others which seem credibly 'American' are just as close to music from much earlier in his career. It is perhaps reasonable to argue that the 'New World' Symphony and 'American' Quartet are 'American' because of their titles and because of the novelty of tone that they adopt, but when it comes to melodic detail and some aspects of atmosphere the issue is by no means clear. Looking beyond the Cello Concerto and Dvořák's American stay we can see many aspects of his 'American' style appearing in works composed when he was safely settled back in Bohemia. The main motif for the eponymous heroine of his penultimate opera *Rusalka* is taken almost unchanged from a sketch made in America (in the sixth American sketchbook); aside from 'American' melodic elements which crop up in the revision to his opera *The Jacobin* (*Jakobín*, op. 84, B 200) and his last opera *Armida* (op. 115, B 206), the directness of utterance which is such a novel feature of the 'New World' Symphony is also apparent in the four symphonic poems based on Erben ballads composed on his return to Prague (B 195–8).

To say that the Cello Concerto is a transitional work back to Dvořák's European style not only implies that the 'American' style was something of an aberration, but is misleading concerning his development as a composer. It is quite evident that 'American' elements occur in work composed at a time when Dvořák's most probable sentiment regarding the New World was one of relief that he was no longer living and working there. The point is that aspects of melody and atmosphere present in the 'American' works persist in later compositions, even if other aspects of style were shifting. In the Cello Concerto, there are, indeed, strong 'American' elements, but they are part of a naturally evolving style of a composer still at the height of his powers and are manifested in a challenging approach to melodic development and form in the first movement, and, as we shall see, more personalised expression in the slow movement and the coda of the finale. But if the Cello Concerto is more adventurous structurally, more personal and less public than the 'New World' Symphony, the 'American' Quartet and the Quintet, this should not conceal the fact that many of the elements that made these works an enormous popular success continued to enrich Dvořák's style up to the very end.

4

'Decisions and revisions': sketch and compositional process

Dvořák's sketches are usually illuminating. In the case of the B minor Cello Concerto the remarkable feature that emerges from a comparison of the continuous sketch and the finished score is the extent to which Dvořák refined his initial thoughts; this was less a question of changing the basic inspiration – the essentials of the thematic fibre are all present in the sketch as are many of the formal details – than of adding a deep level of continuity which, especially in the first movement, gives the finished product an organic quality that is often barely apparent in the somewhat episodic continuous sketch.

Although sketching was an important part of the compositional process for Dvořák, he did not, on the whole, go in for working through multiple versions of ideas in the manner of Beethoven. There are occasions when the evolution of a theme involved him in several attempts – ten in the case of the main theme of the finale of the Eighth Symphony[1] – but these are relatively rare. Nor, for much of his career, are there extensive signs of Dvořák collecting melodic raw material as a preliminary to his continuous sketches. During his two American stays (26 September 1892 to 19 May 1894, and 26 October 1894 to 16 April 1895) this practice began to change. Perhaps owing to the pressure that his teaching and administrative duties placed upon his normal composing practices, Dvořák took to notating ideas for works in a series of seven so-called 'American' sketchbooks for attention when he had more free time to compose. A number of these turned into compositions completed during his American stays; others, like the 'Neptune' Symphony sketched in the summer and autumn of 1893, came to nothing; one, at least – the opening idea for the Sonata for Cello (B 419, see Chapter 2) – was held in reserve for six years before it eventually appeared as Rusalka's motif. In general, rather than refining his ideas away from the consecutive process of composition, Dvořák confined most of the main business of 'working out' to a continuous sketch. But even if he was not a compulsive preliminary sketcher, he could often be a compulsive reviser: five of his eleven operas and four of his nine symphonies, among many other examples, were subjected to very substantial revision and, in an appreciable number of cases, extensive recomposition. Sometimes the changes were made when the composer came back to a work after a number of years with a view to performance or publication, as with his First String Quartet and Second Symphony. On other occasions, Dvořák made changes on the spot during rehearsal – the last two chords of the first movement of the 'New World' Symphony were the product of just this kind of spontaneity.[2]

The case of the Cello Concerto was somewhat different. Dvořák made some relatively slight changes before publication, possibly as a result of his experiences during rehearsals, and Hanuš Wihan made some alterations to the solo part in the composer's manuscript score (not all of which survived to publication; these will be considered in Chapter 7). But by far the most substantial change was made after the work had seemed, to all intents and purposes, complete. The composer's notes on the title page and on the final pages of the completed manuscript reveal the basic details of the revision; they also furnish us with an example of the kind of small domestic detail that often found its way on to the composer's autographs, not to mention revealing his characteristic uncertainty about opus numbers:

Title page
(Seventh composition written in America 1894–1895)/(op. 103) or 104 ('Te Deum', op. 103)/Concerto/ (op. 104)/for/ Violoncello/with orchestral accompaniment/composed by/Antonín Dvořák/Score

Date at the start of the score
New York 18 18/11 94

Note at the end of the first version of the score
Thanks be to God!/ Completed in New York/9 February 1895/ on the birthday of our little Otto/On Saturday morning at 11.30

Note at the end of the revised version of score
I finished the concerto in New York,/but when I returned to /
Bohemia I changed the ending/ completely, as it now stands./ In
Písek 18 11/6 95.[3]

The personal reasons that prompted Dvořák to revise the end of the
Concerto are best dealt with in a consideration of the work's expressive
content (see Chapter 6), but the mechanics of the revision can be laid out
effectively enough below as part of the context of the work's compositional process.

The continuous sketch

The only preliminary material relating to the Concerto which survives
in advance of the continuous sketch was, as we have seen, the idea for the
finale of a cello sonata jotted down in the third American sketchbook in
the summer of 1894 (see Chapter 2: Ex 2.2a). Though extremely embry-
onic, this fragment could well have been more than just the melodic seed
of the finale of the Concerto: it may have influenced Dvořák's original
intention for the key of the work. As it stands in the fifth of the American
sketchbooks, the continuous sketch of the Concerto began and ran for
some thirty-seven bars in D minor, the key of the relevant sketch for the
Cello Sonata, before restarting in B minor, the key of the Concerto as it
now stands.

Dvořák's continuous sketches could take a number of forms. In vocal
works, such as opera or oratorio, the layout might be a vocal line with a
bass, sometimes including figuring to indicate the harmonies. In instrumental music, Dvořák used one or more staves, depending on the level of
accompanimental detail he wished to remember, but more often than not
a single line proved sufficient. To the simple resource of a single staff,
Dvořák would often add designations for specific solo instruments or
orchestral tuttis, occasional harmonic details or suggestions of counterpoint, and verbal prompts, often to remind himself of the tonality –
especially where the key-signature involved large numbers of sharps or
flats – but very little else. Such is the case for much of the twenty-two
pages of continuous sketch for the Cello Concerto which he began in
New York on 8 November 1894.[4]

31

Ex. 4.1(a) and (b)

(a)   [Allegro]

(b)   [Allegro] Grandioso

First movement: Allegro

The D minor 'false-start' of the Concerto (marked Allegro moderato), lacks some of the detail of the second attempt (not least in its decidedly unformed woodwind riposte to the initial clarinet theme (bars 7–8 in the full score)), and the phrasing is painfully four-square, with little of the open-ended quality that makes this initial orchestral tutti in the final version so successful. The restart of the continuous sketch, in B minor of course, shows both a stronger grip on detail and a much clearer sense of direction. Indeed, for the first thirty-one bars, the sketch follows almost exactly the pattern of the finished score. One detail, however, is different and significant: in the continuous sketch the tutti treatment of the main motif repeats the first four bars (with one slight rhythmic alteration) then continues with the same shape on the subdominant, though with a much less convincing melodic alteration in which the melody falls to a D (bar 5) before returning to an E (see Ex. 4.1a); in the finished score Dvořák introduces a melodic variant which by rising to an F-sharp (bar 3) and presenting the scale a third higher, leads much more dynamically to the repetition of the theme on the subdominant chord over a tonic pedal (see Ex. 4.1b). The alteration is crucial to the effective unfolding of the tutti and it is interesting that Dvořák introduces this aspect not in the continuous sketch but in his finished score; much the same is true, as will be seen, of his treatment of the second theme.

The sketch of the remainder of the tutti is far less coherent. A number of remote flat keys (C minor, E-flat major and A-flat major) were assayed and abandoned, as was a more conventional articulation of the dominant built on the main theme just before the soloist's first entry. At its first

Ex. 4.2(a) and (b)

appearance in the continuous sketch, the second theme had crystallised to Dvořák's satisfaction sufficiently for him not to need to make much alteration on the page or to work through variants before coming to the state of the melody that has delighted the world ever since the first performance. Nevertheless, in some subtle ways it is still far from the final form it reached in the finished score, and a comparison of the preliminary and final versions is instructive (see Ex. 4.2a and 4.2b: the last three bars of the reduction of the final form place the violin parts on top, with the less prominent woodwind counterpoint underneath). Immediately striking is the shaping of the theme in the continuous sketch: the sixteen bars of the melody fall into clear four-bar periods until the last five-bar phrase, which nevertheless concludes with a leadenly trite

Ex. 4.3

cadence. The final version of the theme is extended by two bars leading to the lively (Tempo 1) tutti (a feature which did not occur to Dvořák until relatively late in the continuous sketch of the movement), which provides the concluding section of the introduction. The sketch of the theme has none of the subtle internal development of the final version, where Dvořák repeats the descending phrase of bars 9–11 and adds an inspired element of melodic variation to the last appearance of the opening bar (compare the simple repetition of the opening idea in Ex. 4.2a, bar 13, with the final version Ex. 4.2b, bar 15), nor its expressive chromatic shading, amounting, almost, to a form of notated portamento (see Ex. 4.2b, bars 4 and 8). The version of the theme in the continuous sketch, for all the beauty of its opening idea, is damagingly literal with its formal repetitions and closed four-bar phrases. This is, of course, the crucial difference between the continuous sketch and the finished version of the first movement. In frank contradiction of its epithet, the continuous sketch has very little of the sense of continuity and evolution that is such an outstanding feature of the movement; so many aspects of the melodic development of themes were left for the final working out. The sketch of the recapitulation is another case in point: while Dvořák seems to have had no doubt that it would begin with the second subject, its melodic form was not initially the inspired variant that crowns this climactic moment. After a set of what appear to be rising double-stopped sixths from the solo cello and two bars of dominant preparation, it is a recapitulation in B major of the original version of the second subject (see Ex. 4.3);[5] the theme retains its questing second phrase and has none of the finality of the moment in the finished score. (As can be seen from this example it seems to have been Dvořák's intention for the solo cello to

Ex. 4.4(a) and (b)

(a) [Allegro]

(b) [Allegro]

take over from the orchestra after a four-bar tutti – see figure *a* – just as in the final version.)

Of course, numerous other aspects of detail differ between the two sources. Clapham cites an important change in the pointing of the figuration just as the movement reaches the first Tempo 1 marking after the entry of the soloist (bar 110).[6] Dvořák's first thought for the cello's figuration was lacking in the upbeat character which ensures a sense of movement (see Ex. 4.4a). A simple shift of the semiquaver group on to the weak beat provides the necessary impetus (see Ex. 4.4b).

The remarkable passage in A-flat minor at the heart of the development (bar 224 ff.) was extensively prefigured in the sketch, though, as was often the case, Dvořák left out many of the accidentals and provided himself with the key written out (A-flat minor; As moll) as a mnemonic. The preliminary version of the coda again reveals that Dvořák's conception of a gradually evolving movement had yet to crystallise. As in the orchestral introduction, there is the suggestion of a tendency towards flat keys, which in the context of a mature Dvořák sonata movement would have seemed entirely redundant. He also made an attempt to involve the second subject and the brisk concluding figure of the orchestral introduction, but on second thoughts based the coda firmly on the opening subject in a clear B major.

Second movement: Adagio, ma non troppo

Quite often in his larger-scale compositions, Dvořák started work on scoring a movement while he was still sketching it. He had started to

Ex. 4.5(a) and (b)

(a) Lento

(b) Adagio, ma non troppo

score the first movement on 18 November and he completed it on 12 December, just a day after the end date of the sketch ('18 11/12 94'). He must have started work on the slow movement (marked Lento rather than the Adagio, ma non troppo it became in the finished score) almost immediately since it was completed and ready for scoring by 15 December, a task which took him until 30 December. Some indication of the rapidity with which he worked once the basics of the outline were secure is given by the fact that he went back to recast the coda of the first movement while sketching the opening section of the slow movement; thus revision and scoring of the last portion of the first movement must have been done in hardly more than two working days.

As with the thematic material of the first movement, much of the outline of the opening melody of the Adagio, ma non troppo is present at the opening of the continuous sketch, although it lacks the graceful shaping of the final version (cf. Exx. 4.5a and 4.5b). Dvořák did little to alter the ordering of events in this opening section in his final version. In both, the solo cello enters at bar 9, although in the sketch it lacks the upbeat of the final version; here also Dvořák confirms the implied modulation to B minor in bar 7 which he cancelled in the final version with a graceful side-slip back to G major. The subsidiary theme played by clarinets in thirds (bar 15 ff.) is also present in the sketch, written in a neater, more decisive hand and with far fewer corrections than in the opening bars. As in his sketch of the first movement, Dvořák restarted that of the slow movement. While aspects of the phrasing come closer to the final version, Dvořák's recasting of the opening theme takes it much further from the original sketch for which, with one or two alterations, he ultimately opted.

Ex. 4.6(a.i), (a.ii), (b) and (c)

(a.i)   Andante

(a.ii)   Allegro

(b)   [Adagio, ma non troppo]
        Tempo I

(c)

Solo
cello

molto espress.

Dvořák's first thought for the G minor opening of the central section of the Adagio, ma non troppo (bar 65 ff.) could be read, with its stepwise rise through a third and fall back on to the tonic, as a cyclic reference to the opening theme of the first movement (see Ex. 4.6a); it is possible that this impulse may have arisen from a desire for overt unity at this relatively early stage in the Concerto's development, or it may merely reflect the fact that the first movement's powerful thematic presence was still fresh in his mind. A minimal alteration in the final version (Ex. 4.6b), however, not only covers the resemblance but neatly adumbrates the descending phrase of the subsequent theme (Ex. 4.6c). Dvořák's introduction of the second verse of his song 'Lasst mich allein!' ('Leave me alone!'), the first of four settings of German poetry (later translated into Czech by V. J. Novotný op. 82, B 157), provides the continuation of the central section. His decision to make use of the song and its emotional significance to him will be dealt with in Chapter 6, but Dvořák's deft transformation of the theme, with its strongly characterised word rhythms, is worth noting, as is the fact that he took trouble to retain the original bitter-sweet harmony of the song's second verse.

The rather rudimentary form of the sketch for the return of the opening material in the slow movement is perhaps an indication of the speed at which Dvořák worked. The recapitulation in the sketch is damagingly short and there is little indication of the richness of the cello's *quasi Cadenza* (bar 107 ff.) that is present in the final version with its accompanying woodwind detail. In fact, although Dvořák had intended that the cello adopt double-stopping at this point, the passage did not reach a final form until after he had completed the score (see Chapter 7). Clearly, much of the work on the movement went on during the creation of the full score on which Dvořák was engaged for the rest of December.

Third movement, finale: Allegro moderato

An early sketch for the finale (made on 16 November) shows the outline of an introduction similar to the one that now exists, but Dvořák did not set to work in earnest on the movement until New Year's Day 1895. Having made a brief preliminary sketch, his treatment of the work in the continuous sketch shows little uncertainty of touch in the introduction; there was clearly no need to restart work, as he had done with the first two movements. Much of what is contained in the continuous sketch follows the shape of the finale before the later revision; if anything, there are times when the sketch includes more material than Dvořák felt was necessary, including a rather laboured approach to the orchestral statement of the main theme after the first episode. The development of the melodic material for the Poco meno mosso episode (bar 143 ff.) in the continuous sketch is an interesting example of ornamental accretion followed by rationalisation. The original thought is telegraphically simple (see Ex. 4.7a); the first attempt at variation was clearly too complex (see Ex. 4.7b), almost an ornament too far. Dvořák's 'solution' reduces the sextuplet to a group of four semiquavers and gives it a more distinctive melodic profile (see Ex. 4.7c).

The impressive degree of fluency which Dvořák built up as he worked on the sketch of this movement is indicated by the transition to the Moderato episode in G major (bar 281 ff.), which grows with superb naturalness out of the quintuplet figure at the end of the main subject in the previous ritornello: repeated *fortissimo*, it descends through the strings, evening out into four semiquavers before forming the quaver

Ex. 4.7(a), (b) and (c)

introduction to the approach to the new thematic material. The essence of this flowing G major melody also gave Dvořák relatively little difficulty, although some of the subsequent passagework tended towards an overly complex tonal scheme, which did not survive into the final version.

The lead up to the return to the tonic major did not reach its final form until Dvořák scored the Concerto. As it stands, the move to B major (bar 347 ff.) is preceded by an eight-bar passage in B-flat which descends via an A flat bass (spelt enharmonically as G-sharp) to a six-four on the new tonic; in the sketch, Dvořák remained on the C-sharp major (spelt enharmonically as D-flat) which preceded the B-flat passage in the final version. The movement of the bass in the sketch is not clear, but the insertion of the word 'Fis' (F-sharp) at the point when the key changes to B major might well be an indication that he intended to settle on a second inversion of the tonic, as he does in the final version. What he must have recognised when he came to scoring the passage was that the change from D-flat to B major, though attractive, has little of the conclusive quality of the fall from B-flat to B major on which he eventually settled.

The sketch becomes less conclusive as the ending of the movement approaches, though Dvořák put a line under these preliminary efforts with the note: 'prvý konec poslední věty' ('first ending of the last movement'). This was not quite the end, however. Some more ideas noted down after this 'first ending' show that Dvořák continued to ruminate on the conclusion, mainly with a view to providing a meditative extension of the tonic chord, much as occurs in the finished work at bar 457. In a descending sequence of minims there is also a suggestion, examined further below, of the inspiring chord sequence that closes the Concerto in Dvořák's revised conclusion, but no indication of the final version of the coda with its explicit quotations.

The revision

Dvořák completed the first version of the score on 9 February 1895. The personal reasons that prompted him to return to the work (which was finally completed on 6 June 1895) will be assessed in Chapter 6, but as it stands the original ending must have seemed somewhat perfunctory. A crude comparison of the number of bars in the coda of the original and revised versions, forty as opposed to ninety-five, gives some indication of the drastic nature of the extension. In performance terms the new coda adds between two minutes and one second, in the fastest recorded performance (Feuermann/Taube, 1929), and two minutes and forty-eight seconds, in the slowest (Rostropovich/Giulini, 1978).[7]

The appreciable lengthening of the finale not only gave Dvořák the opportunity to introduce quotations from previous movements, but also to provide a conclusion that complements both the extent and the gravity of the previous movements. It would be hard to imagine the work without its reminiscences of the first and second movements, so suggestive of extra-musical content, and yet it is not unreasonable to speculate that Dvořák considered extending the coda even before he considered including the cyclic features. No sketch material survives for the reminiscences, but the additional material after the end of the continuous sketch includes elements that were used in the revised conclusion. The extra material contains two ideas: the first prefigures the solo cello's gradual rise towards a top B (bars 457 ff.), though without any hint of the reminiscences of the first subject of the opening movement which occur between bars 461 and 465. The second idea, on two staves, is a descending sequence of minims under a pedal B (see Ex. 4.8); if, as would be normal with Dvořák's sketches, these notes indicate possible bass movement, it would seem that he was already beginning to feel his way towards the progression on which he eventually settled for the Andante maestoso and the Allegro vivo concluding bars (497 ff.): the much more satisfactory replacement for the banal repeated B major 'in tempo' which

Ex. 4.8

connected so perfunctorily with bar 453 in the first version. While Clapham attributes Dvořák's 'strong urge to make a complete change in the conclusion of the Concerto's finale'[8] to his reaction to the death of Josefina, his sister-in-law, we cannot exclude the possibility that there were also sound musical reasons for Dvořák's change to this conclusion – not least to avoid an abrupt and under-weighted close – and that he had been considering this possibility even before the bereavement.

5

The score I: forms and melodies

A symphonic concerto?

There is widespread consensus among commentators that the Cello Concerto is the most successful of Dvořák's works in the form. Indeed, the essential 'rightness' of the piece, and in particular its opening orchestral tutti, is often established in relation to a perceived lack of success in his Piano and Violin Concertos. For Alec Robertson, with the Cello Concerto Dvořák had 'got concerto form just where he wanted it'.[1] Robertson rarely gave wholehearted approval for any work by Dvořák in his Master Musicians study of the composer; for him the first movement of the Violin Concerto was 'Too long for an introduction to the extensive slow movement' and 'too short for what is called first-movement form',[2] and the Piano Concerto 'has not so much a warm heart as cold feet'.[3] In the case of the Cello Concerto, Robertson presumably felt he was on safer ground in praising the work, since he immediately follows his complimentary introduction to it with Brahms's reaction as recounted to Tovey by the German cellist, Robert Hausmann: 'Why on earth didn't I know that one could write a Violoncello Concerto like this? If I had only known, I would have written one long ago!'[4]

Alongside the general approval rating for the Cello Concerto is a widely held perception that it is both symphonic and something of a return to earlier, presumably pre-American period, practices. In *A Companion to the Concerto*,[5] Joan Chissell places the Cello Concerto in 'The Symphonic Concerto' division of the chapter entitled 'The Concerto after Beethoven'. Robert Layton, the editor of the anthology, has no hesitation in advancing the symphonic credentials of the Concerto in his own study of the work:

The Cello Concerto . . . has all the virtues of its predecessor [the Violin Concerto] together with a mastery of formal design that distinguishes only his greatest compositions like the D minor Symphony. Indeed, the opening exposition has been compared with that of the Symphony, and it is worth noting that the sketch of the Concerto originally started life in this key.[6]

It was John Clapham who first made this comparison, and his lead has been followed by nearly all English and American commentators on the work.[7] A more reflective assessment comes from David Beveridge, but even he is inclined to see a return to an excellence characteristic of Dvořák's works prior to his stay in America, stating: 'When, after a year's respite, he again took up sonata form in his B minor Cello Concerto, it was with a resolve to reinfuse the form with some of the richness and complexity of his earlier masterpieces'.[8]

The clear message in these judgements is that the Concerto looks back to the tried and tested norms of symphonic composition which Dvorak had adopted in his Sixth and Seventh Symphonies. Evident also is the sense that Dvořák was reverting to a more evidently Austro-German mode of development, something more recognisably Brahmsian. Dvořák's signal admiration for Brahms is certainly not at issue – even as he was at work on scoring the slow movement of the Concerto he wrote a heartfelt letter of thanks to Brahms for proofreading a number of his works, a task he was unable to undertake owing to distance;[9] nor does any writer go so far as to finger the Concerto as Brahmsian, as they were inclined to with earlier works, notably the Sixth Symphony. But implicit in many commentaries is the feeling that the work is a return to a perceptible orthodoxy after the 'Simplistic Extreme', to quote Beveridge, of the American works. And it is an orthodoxy of which, if we are to believe Hausmann's story as told by Tovey (and nearly every non-Czech commentator since seems to have), Brahms approved.

Czech commentaries on the Concerto, though untrammelled by a need to establish Dvořák's credentials by comparing him with Brahms, also often allude to its symphonic qualities. Berkovec states that the Concerto 'could well be described as a concertante-symphony',[10] reflecting Šourek's view that in essence the work, while not limiting the effectiveness of the solo part, was composed in a symphonic manner. In support of this, he refers with approval to Karel Knittl's early judgement of the

Concerto from the periodical *Dalibor*, stating: 'Rightly it was written that this is in fact a three-movement symphony with obbligato cello'.[11]

But are these images of the orthodox, symphonic concerto justified? Karel Hoffmeister, in an important early study of the composer, speaks about the work's symphonic scoring, but introduces another strand: 'The Concerto for Violoncello, although it perhaps belongs to the period when his ideas were rather co-ordinated than developed, remains one of the finest works in the whole literature of the 'cello, if not by its intellectual side, at least by its rhythmic qualities, its intoxicating melodies, so well adapted to the character of the solo instrument, and its richly coloured, symphonic scoring'.[12] Hoffmeister's description of the Concerto as coming from the 'period when his ideas were rather co-ordinated than developed' seems to fly in the face of the wisdom of succeeding commentators, with their tendency to focus on the composition's symphonic qualities, but it deserves consideration, not least because it echoes the reaction of two of the first critics of the work. The reviewer of the première of the Concerto for *The Times* referred to: 'a certain diffuseness arising from the composer's prodigality in themes',[13] while the critic of *The Musical Times* went so far as to suggest that: 'We are by no means sure that, as a Violoncello Concerto, this work will become a favourite, and it had better be regarded, perhaps, as three orchestral movements with violoncello obbligato'.[14] Looked at superficially, the work could well be construed as somewhat episodic. One only needs to consider the second subject in the opening Allegro, almost song-like in its lyricism and given to one of the most vocally expressive solo instruments, the horn; the nature of the theme and the almost operatic manner in which it is introduced into the first movement are unique in Dvořák's output, features which have had a considerable effect on performance practice. Recordings from the last forty years show an increasing tendency for conductors to emphasise the separateness of this passage from the rest of the movement, enhancing its song-like quality by slowing the tempo far more than Dvořák's Molto sostenuto ($\downarrow = 100$).[15] Similarly, the development, with its essentially lyrical demeanour and, above all, at its centre the melodic transformation of the first subject presented as a duet between the solo cello and flute (bars 225–39) has no parallel in any other first movement development by the composer. As with the first appearance of the second subject, this

Ex. 5.1

episode – no other word will do – is prepared in a way that sets it apart from the texture of the rest of the movement, almost as if it is an aria, a 'still centre' at the very heart of the movement (see Ex. 5.1); its inward quality and avoidance of a strong sense of movement (in fact, the counterpoint in the flute part, with its almost improvisatory reaction to the cello solo, seems bent on retarding forward motion), compounded by the doubling of the note values of the first subject, seem almost a contradiction of the very nature of symphonic development as Dvořák himself had practised it up to that time. All of these features set this movement apart from anything comparable in Dvořák's symphonic output, not least the opening movement of the Seventh Symphony, with which it is so often compared.

The epithet symphonic is, of course, also frequently used to characterise the concertos of Brahms, partly as a recognition of their large-scale qualities, but also to typify the musical discourse.[16] But comparison between Dvořák's methods in the Cello Concerto and those of Brahms in his concertos, all of which Dvořák would have known by 1894, reveal little congruence beyond a tendency to extend the end of the opening phrase in the first movement by repetition and sequence during the early stages of the work (see Cello Concerto, first movement, bars 11–17); here Dvořák might have been looking to Brahms as a model, in particular to passages early in the first movements of the Violin Concerto and the Second Piano Concerto (see Brahms's Violin Concerto, first movement, bars 31–41, and his Second Piano Concerto, first movement, bars 31–5), but in essence this short-term developmental practice was already well established as part of his compositional armoury.

The first movement: thematic variation and metamorphosis

If Dvořák's first movement and much of the rest of the Concerto is not conventionally symphonic, it is certainly powerfully coherent, even given the presence of the formal unorthodoxy of beginning a recapitulation with the second subject. Table 5.1 gives some idea of the lucidity of Dvořák's design in the first movement and the role of key and theme in a general progression from B minor to B major.

While the artificiality of tabular presentation might seem in danger of confirming Hoffmeister's view that the work is 'rather co-ordinated than developed',[17] it does serve to point up the extraordinary tonal consistency of the movement. The slow progress of broad blocks of tonality gives the movement a strong sense of epic development. The only extensive excursions away from keys close to the tonic and relative major occur in the approach to the heart of the development with its 'still centre' in

Table 5.1

First movement: *Allegro*		
Orchestral exposition	bars 1–86	First-subject area to bar 56; B minor (see Ex. 5.3a). Second-subject area: bars 57–74; D major (see Ex. 4.2b). Concluding subject: bars 75–86 (not repeated); D major.
Solo exposition	bars 87–204	First subject: bars 87–109 (*Quasi improvisando*); B major/minor. First subject: bars 110–39 (Tempo 1); B minor. Second subject: bars 140–57; D major. Transition (bars 158–65) leading to new idea in F-sharp major (bars 166–9); further transition (bars 170–86) eventually dominated by diminution of first half of opening bar (bars 186–91). Concluding orchestral tutti (bars 192–203); D major.
Development	bars 204–66	Three episodes based on variants of the first subject: (a) bars 204–23: modulating away from D major through C minor, G minor and E-flat minor in preparation for (b) bars 224–39: Molto sostenuto ('still centre' of development); A-flat minor/G-sharp minor (see Ex. 5.1). (c) bars 240–66: modulating towards dominant chord on F-sharp (reached at bar 256, held until bar 266) in preparation for:
Recapitulation	bars 267–318	Second subject: full orchestra followed by solo cello; B major. Near exact repeat of bars 158–91 at bars 285–318 leading to:
Coda	bars 319–54	First subject: full orchestra and solo cello; B major

A-flat minor (changed enharmonically a third of the way through to G-sharp minor); even the move towards the dominant in preparation for the recapitulation is managed in a succinct sixteen bars. The more or less exact repetition in the recapitulation, a minor third lower, of the passage succeeding the second subject in the exposition means that the new theme, originally assayed in the dominant (F-sharp major) at bars 166–7

Ex. 5.2

now occurs in E-flat major (bars 293–7), but this is virtually the only move to a key remote from near relatives of the basic tonality. While Dvořák avoids monotony by a combination of harmonic ornament, lyricism and an astonishing variety of orchestral texture, the relative lack of volatility in modulation, coupled to the extreme regularity of the recapitulation after the quotation of the second theme, adds greatly to the sense of grandeur and gravity projected in the movement.

This atmosphere of weighty inevitability is felt at its strongest in the recapitulation. Dvořák's alteration to the shape of the second subject (cf. Ex. 5.2 with Ex. 4.2b) is designed to give it full impact in its role as a culmination – an effect much enhanced by its full orchestral treatment with festive trumpet fanfares – but his preparation for the moment of recapitulation is also calculated to produce maximum effect. Not only does he settle on the dominant ten bars before the recapitulation, he increases the tension in the approach to the resolution on to the tonic chord with an oscillating, minor-ninth figuration in the cello part three bars before the return (see Ex. 5.2). Amazingly, Šourek identifies the start of the recapitulation as coinciding with the arrival of the A-flat minor episode (Ex. 5.1), despite the later triumphant return to the tonic.[18] By contrast, the similar places in the first movements of his previous three symphonies – to cite works composed in the ten years previous to the Concerto – are both more succinct and surprising.

It is also clear from Table 5.1 that the use of the second subject, with its marked lyrical accent, is restricted to its exposition and appearance as the crown of the recapitulation. The placing of the second subject at this point, while always recognised as unconventional, is invariably praised as a masterstroke. Tovey describes the manoeuvre in particularly fulsome terms as '"short-circuiting" [the movement's] development and recapitulation.' ' The success is brilliant', he went on, 'both in form and in dramatic expression; and the total impression left by the movement is unequivocally that of a masterpiece', adding somewhat defensively, 'whatever the theorists may say'.[19] But the impression left by the recapitulation is less one of surprise at its unconventionality when seen against the norms of sonata practice, even after seventy years of post-Classical experiment, than of extraordinary 'rightness'. As we have seen from the continuous sketch, Dvořák seems to have no doubt that the second subject would initiate the recapitulation, also that it would be in the major key. After a development dominated almost exclusively by the first subject and a profoundly evocative episode in a remote minor key, the return marked both by the second theme *and* the major key could hardly be more conclusive, and it is unparalleled in any of Dvořák's major orchestral works.

While the second subject provides points of stasis and reflection in the exposition and recapitulation, the main engine of forward motion in the movement is provided by the first subject. For a composer with a fondness for the melodic elaboration of his main material, it is perhaps no surprise to find a high degree of variation in his handling of the first subject, but it goes a good deal further than the fortuitously ornamental practices found in earlier works. Dvořák's treatment of his first subject seems in many places to be related to an evolutionary view of sonata

Ex. 5.3(a), (b), (c), (d), (e), (f) and (g)

(a)   Allegro

(b)   [Allegro]

Quasi improvisando

(c)   [Allegro]
Grandioso

(d)   [Allegro]
In tempo, grandioso

(e)   Allegro]

(f)   Tempo I

(g)   [Allegro]

style expressed through the change from a somewhat reticent modally inflected B minor to a triumphant B major. This is not a manifestation of Lisztian thematic metamorphosis in which the often tortuously chromatic elements of a theme are 'ironed out' to create an aspiring chorale-like variant (for example, the first movement of Liszt's *Eine Faust-Symphonie*; cf. the first theme of the opening Lento assai with the melody at score letter O (Eulenburg score), Grandioso, poco meno mosso).[20] Instead, the process in Dvořák's first movement leads to changes to the theme which are relatively slight but, nevertheless, have considerable structural impact. Dvořák's first major change to the opening theme comes with the initial entry of the soloist (cf. Ex. 5.3a and 5.3b). While striking and boldly rhetorical in effect, the raising of the minor to a major third might also be construed as a signal of his intention to conclude in the major key, despite retaining the flattened seventh of the original. Unsurprisingly, the theme as presented at the start of the concluding orchestral tutti of the exposition also outlines a major third, but in order to facilitate the wind-down to the development, Dvořák introduces a slide on to the seventh of the D major chord in the second bar of the theme (see Ex. 5.3c). The most far-reaching exploration of the first theme in an explicit form is, of course, the A-flat minor episode in the development (see Ex. 5.1 above), but the most conclusive transformation comes, as the clinching gesture of the whole movement, at the start of the coda. Confirming his intention to conclude the movement in the major key, the theme not only outlines the major third, but, in festive perorational mood, sharpens the previously flattened seventh (see Ex. 5.3d) and, in marked contrast to previous extensions of the theme, its first two bars are followed by a celebratory rising scale.

The 'user-friendly' design of the main theme goes beyond its ability to articulate main structural and tonal features. Dvořák's educational background (in many ways little different from his eighteenth-century Czech predecessors) and a lifetime of compositional practice had given him an ability to manipulate small baroque-style figures to full effect.[21] A diminution of the opening idea adds greatly to the impetus of the solo cello's leading role at Tempo 1 (bar 110) after its first entry. Yet another diminution adds considerable urgency to the start of the development section (see Ex. 5.3e), its tight dactylic character (marked 'x' in the example) imparting motivic identity to the rising diminished

Ex. 5.4

arpeggio at bar 210.[22] But beyond Dvořák's recognition of the developmental potential inherent in the design of his main melody is an ability to extend his material with an improvisational skill amounting to genius. Notable examples include the extension of the cello solo's diminution of the opening idea four bars after the start of the passage beginning at bar 110 (see Ex. 5.3f) and, in the orchestral exposition, the softening of outline as the first theme is drawn into the transition towards the second subject (see Ex. 5.3g). Still more remarkable is the inspired extension of the first theme which, with the cello's arrival at the second subject in the solo exposition, introduces an elegant curving phrase whose rise and fall pre-echoes the outline of the new theme (see Ex. 5.4).

A slightly different order of thematic variation occurs in the third episode of the development, where Dvořák takes the opening two beats of the first subject and extends them with an appoggiatura figure; he raises the temperature as the development approaches the dominant preparation for the recapitulation by turning the original leisurely crotchet triplet augmentation into a pair of quavers (see Ex. 5.5a and 5.5b). In his discussion of an apparently new melody for cello which occurs in the recapitulation of the first movement of the 'American' Quartet (bars 123–7) Alan Houtchens invokes Schoenberg's concept of 'developing variation';[23] in many ways Schoenberg's description of the practice as a 'way of altering something given, so as to develop further its component parts as well as the figures built from them, the outcome always being something new, with an apparently low degree of resemblance to its

Ex. 5.5(a) and (b)

prototype'[24] seems entirely appropriate for Dvořák's treatment of his first theme at this point in the first movement of the Cello Concerto.

Apart from its developmental and generative aspects, the first theme, notably its first two bars, fulfils another purpose. The return of the theme at the end of the Concerto will be examined more fully in the next chapter, but this cyclic dimension is not the only pointer to its function as a motto. The motivic aspects of the first theme are carried mainly by its opening two bars. The remainder of the melody is treated much more fluidly; as we have seen, its general tendency to fall is contradicted in the movement's cheerful peroration. For the most part the opening of the theme retains its strongly characterised identity to the extent that occasionally in the first movement the appearance of this theme seems to have an effect beyond the purely abstract; a notable place is at the end of the flute solo in the A–flat minor/G–sharp minor episode in the development whose improvisatory rapture is crowned by a concluding reference to the opening two bars (see Ex. 5.1, bar 15).

It would be wrong to conclude a consideration of this extraordinary movement without some reference to its debt to the composer's earlier practices, in particular to the Piano and Violin Concertos. In the wind-down to the first solo entry in the Cello Concerto Dvořák may well have had in mind the conclusion of the orchestral exposition of his Piano Concerto, with its similarly ominous drum roll reinforced by brass (cf. the Piano Concerto, first movement, bars 62–5 with the Cello Concerto, first movement, bars 84–6). He may also have been prompted to adopt a cadenza-like aspect in the first entry of the soloist in the Cello Concerto by the example of the opening of his Violin Concerto, where there is a similarly rhetorical passage for the soloist before the main business of the movement gets underway. But these are small points which do nothing to detract from the assurance and frank novelty of this first movement. It is always tempting, and sometimes quite erroneous, to clinch the case for a work's transcendent excellence by a claim of uniqueness, but from so many points of view – formal, tonal, expressive, rhetorical and emotional – this movement stands aside from his symphonic style as it had developed up to this time. And given its evident success from nearly every standpoint, it will always remain a remarkable monument to the creative fertility of Dvořák's maturity.

Second movement: Adagio, ma non troppo

One aspect of the Concerto on which the main commentators at its première were agreed was the excellence of the slow movement. The critic of *The Musical Times* described it as 'the gem of the work';[25] the lordly reviewer of *The Athenaeum*, wearied, it seems, by the length of a concert which rendered him powerless to give a full assessment of the work, was able, nevertheless, to venture the opinion that: 'at any rate the middle movement, *adagio, ma non troppo*, in G, may be pronounced worthy of the Bohemian composer'.[26] While castigating its 'excessive length', the critic of *The Times* concurred that the slow movement was 'very beautiful'.[27] The extraordinary lyrical beauty of the movement is couched in a relatively uncomplicated modified ternary frame (see Table 5.2), but its simplicity of outline should not be confused with a simplistic approach to thematic transformation.

In this superbly sustained Adagio, ma non troppo, as with the outstandingly lyrical Largo of the 'New World' Symphony, Dvořák did not attempt the developmental density of the slow movements of his Sixth and Seventh Symphonies, nor the near-seamless span of the Adagio of the Eighth. Even so, despite the clearly sectional nature of the movement, there is a great deal of subtlety in the treatment of themes across the principal divisions. Apart from the way in which Dvořák prepares for and treats the transformation of the song quotation in the central section, there are a number of expressive variations which affect the mood. One of the most explicit of these is employed to mark the return to

Table 5.2

Second movement: Adagio, ma non troppo		
Opening section	bars 1–38	First theme: woodwind, bars 1–8; G major (see Ex. 4.5b). Cello solo modification of first theme, bars 9–14; G major. New theme: woodwind, trombones and solo cello, bars 15–21; G major (see Ex. 5.6a). Elaboration, initially based on first theme: solo cello, woodwind and strings, bars 21–34 (see Ex. 5.6b); modulatory, eventually cadencing in G major in preparation for:
Central section	bars 39–94	Introduction (G minor): full orchestra, bars 39–42 (see Ex. 4.6b), followed by transformation of song, 'Lasst mich allein!', for solo cello (see Ex. 4.6c), bars 42–9; modulating from G minor to B-flat major; oboe and flute take up a further variant of the song, bars 49–57; Un poco più animato, bars 57–64, leads back to repeat of full orchestra introduction to central section and further variants of the song, bars 65–94, in preparation for:
Final section (return)	bars 95–166	Opening theme in brass, bars 95–107; G major. *Quasi cadenza*, solo cello joined by flute, bassoon and clarinet, bars 107–28; G major. Return of second theme from bars 15–21, G major, with further elaboration leading to:
Coda	bars 149–66	Reduced orchestra and solo cello; G major.

the opening theme at bar 95, where it is played by horns with the cellos and basses providing a march-like rhythmic accompaniment; here the transformation is effected by skilful orchestration and suggestive rhythmic underpinning. Even more remarkable than this, since it involves subtle melodic change as well as captivating instrumentation and rhythmic variation, is a transformation that initiates the start of the coda.

Ex. 5.6(a) and (b)

(a) [Adagio, ma non troppo]

(b) [Adagio, ma non troppo]

Ex. 5.7

Here, over a rising line in the solo cello, the flute plays a remote, but still identifiable, transformation of the hectoring G minor melody which opens the central section; by ornamenting the outline of the theme with turns and setting it over an extended G major pedal, the funereal roar that heralded the song quotation earlier in the movement is turned into a moment of exquisite pastoral repose (cf. Ex. 5.7 and Ex. 4.6b above).[28]

The introduction of the song 'Lasst mich allein!' ('Leave me alone!'), though a moment of signal beauty, does not bring with it any sense of disjunction. Although it is, strictly speaking, an 'imported' element, it does not seem like an interloper. Clapham implies that Dvořák was prompted to include the song during the composition of the slow movement as the result of a letter from his sister-in-law Josefina Kaunitzová,[29] but the result feels less like a quotation than a perfectly natural melodic addition. There can be little doubt that the song was a specific choice (see Chapter 6), and yet it seems entirely at ease with the surrounding material in the slow movement. None of the earlier reviewers, for instance, drew attention to it as a disparate 'added' element. The reason for its successful integration into the fabric of the Adagio, ma non troppo could well be that Dvořák had considered making use of it from the outset of the sketch of his movement rather than during the compositional process. Josefina's letter is dated 26 November 1894 and Dvořák did not begin work on the sketch, as we have seen, until he had completed the first movement on 12 December. The period of sixteen days from the date at the head of the letter would have been ample time for it to reach Dvořák in New York, and there is good evidence that he had received it by 7 December,[30] thus allowing him to take into account his use of the song when working on the movement as a whole. The essential character of the melody is based on falling sequences after an initial rise – an octave in the original song, a third in the continuous sketch and a fifth in the finished score (see Ex. 4.6c). While these characteristics are not particularly marked in the opening theme of the slow movement, the subsequent melody for clarinets (starting at bar 15) does seem to reflect something of the outline of the song (cf. Ex. 4.6c above and Ex. 5.6a). Moreover, the solo cello's affecting approach to the central section, built as a counterpoint to a line in the violas based on the first bar of the opening theme, also shadows the general contours of the song (Ex. 5.6b; similar material is used later at bar 60 ff. and also bar 86 ff.), as does the stentorian opening of the central section – a fortuitous alteration, as has already been noted in Chapter 4 (see Ex. 4.6b). Thus, by the time 'Lasst mich allein!' appears, with its original time-signature changed from common time to the $\frac{3}{4}$ of the Adagio, ma non troppo, it is not just integrated – its outline has already suffused much of what has gone before.

For a work that many have supposed to be something of a turning away from Dvořák's 'American' style, the parallels with his 'New World' manner in this slow movement in particular are remarkably strong. The general pastoral mood of much of it has already been noted, but there are more specific resemblances to be found with the Largo of the 'New World' Symphony: a broad opening major section followed by a more haunted minor-key central episode is but one. More specific by way of parallel is the frank eruption of woodwind sound during the solo cello's *quasi Cadenza* passage from bar 107 (see Chapter 6 below), an exact equivalent to the entry of the woodwind in the 'New World' Symphony's Largo at bar 90 (a passage which Beckerman has equated with the singing of birds in Longfellow's *Hiawatha* in his discussion of the programmatic background to the Largo[31]). Undoubtedly these picturesque aspects enhance the movement's popularity, but its standing as one of Dvořák's most beautiful, and according to the first critics this judgement was made from the work's première, has as much to do with the benefit its ravishing content derives from the clarity of formal outline.

Finale: Allegro moderato

Dvořák did not add the word 'Rondo' to the designation of his finale, but it is one of his most overt examples of the form. However, despite the consistent returns of the main theme, there are aspects of both form and tonality in this movement, as in the opening Allegro, ma non troppo, which are by no means conventional (see Table 5.3).

As can be seen from the tabular presentation of the movement, the formal propriety of the rondo falls away from about bar 315. Given the generous proportions of the movement up to the second episode, some sort of rationalisation or 'short-circuiting', to borrow Tovey's coinage, was certainly desirable. Dvořák does not repeat his first episode (*B*) and instead of returning to the rondo theme in the tonic immediately after the second episode (*C*), he supplies a magnificently orchestrated presentation of *C* in B major. Not only is the short-circuiting reminiscent of his practice in the first movement, the resemblance is further heightened by the decision to crown the return to the tonic, not with the first theme but with the major and most memorable secondary idea. His approach to tonality exhibits the same evolutionary tendency as in the first movement: just as the B major recapitulation signals the start of the triumphant conclusion of the first movement, without any return to the minor, so the conclusive return to B major in the finale points the way to a similar close. Dvořák's instincts in the peroration to the rondo

Table 5.3

Third movement: Allegro moderato		
Introduction	bars 1–32	Strings and horns followed by full orchestra; B minor, leading to:
Rondo theme A	bars 33–48	Solo cello followed by orchestra; B minor.
Subsidiary idea A1	bars 48–72	Solo cello and reduced orchestra; D major (see Ex. 1.1b) modulating to B minor as a lead back to:
A	bars 73–86	Solo cello and orchestra; B minor.
Transition A2	bars 87–142	Tutti followed by accompanied solo cello; B minor modulating to D major in preparation for:
First episode B	bars 143–76	Solo cello and reduced orchestra (Poco meno mosso; see Ex. 4.7c above); D major.
	bars 177–203	Link for solo cello with minimal accompaniment (Tempo 1) to:
A2	bars 204–45	Tutti followed by accompanied solo cello; D major modulating to B minor in preparation for:
A	bars 246–68	Solo cello followed by full orchestra; B minor.
	bars 269–80	Transition, reduced orchestra, modulating to G major in preparation for:
Second episode C	bars 281–314	Solo cello, reduced orchestra; G major.
	bars 315–46	Transition, solo cello and reduced orchestra modulating to B major in preparation for:
C	bars 347–80	Solo violin, solo cello and reduced orchestra; B major leading to:
A	bars 381–420	Full orchestra and solo cello; B major leading to:
Coda (B major)	bars 421–60	Solo cello, reduced orchestra.
	bars 461–96	Solo cello, reduced orchestra; including quotations from movements 1 and 2 (Andante).
	bars 497–515	Full orchestra: Andante maestoso leading to concluding Allegro vivo.

before the coda are entirely sound; instead of quoting the rondo theme in full in the major key, a feature that might have slowed the movement fatally, he repeats its second bar, seizing on it as a means of initiating an excitable, often sequential, dash to the solemn brass chords which announce the coda. This process, so like that in the latter parts of the first movement, is strikingly at variance with his practice in more recent minor-key symphonic finales. In both the Seventh and the Ninth Symphonies (in D minor and E minor, respectively) Dvořák held on to minor-key versions of his principal theme until very late in the movement, followed by fairly succinct, if brilliantly positive, assertions of the major key. In the outer movements of the Cello Concerto, his business seems to have been the gradual achieving of the major mode, and in the finale he crowns this novel success with the longest *tierce de Picardie* of his mature orchestral career.

Although the formal divisions in the rondo are fairly well differentiated, with clear transitions and lead-backs to the main theme, there is a substratum made up of more subtle features linking a number of the musical ideas. The cheerfully robust subsidiary idea to the first theme shares its phrase structure and also, effectively, its opening rising fourth (see Ex. 1.1b). More intriguingly, a counterpoint to the main theme associated with its first and second appearances seems to provide some of the fibre for a later transition for full orchestra followed by the solo cello (cf. Ex. 5.8a with Ex. 5.8b; see Table 5.3, *Transition A2*).

The use of a steady march rhythm to initiate the finale and underpin its main idea has no parallel in Dvořák's mature symphonic works (its determined mood is something to which we will return in the next chapter). The character is quite unlike the fast-paced, march-like finales of the First and Fourth Symphonies, and seems to have little in common with the more moderately paced *alla marcia* sections in the third movement of the First Symphony (bar 102 ff.) or at the heart of the Adagio of the Third Symphony (bar 98 ff.); nor does its character seem to be looking back to the Moderato, quasi marcia of the D minor Serenade (op. 44, B 77) or even – to cite a work composed only slightly more than a year before the Cello Concerto – the exuberantly flag-waving Allegro giusto, tempo di marcia in *The American Flag* (op. 103, B 177). Once again, Dvořák has supplied us with an orchestral movement that is unique in character, with no obvious precursors in his output. But

Ex. 5.8(a), (b.i), (b.ii)

despite this lack of an obvious precedent, Dvořák handles it with enormous panache at a time when more than one of his finales have occasioned criticism (see below). There is abundant contrast, not least between the energy of the opening two-thirds and the reflective stasis of so much of the concluding portion. Dvořák even manages to create a sense of impetus in the more lyrical sections. Unlike the first movement, the more restful first and second episodes nevertheless maintain an impetus that leads naturally to the returns of the main rondo theme. Apart from these broader considerations, Dvořák's handling of texture and harmony is also remarkable. To cite just two examples: the first episode, while clearly in the relative major, sits on yearningly attractive dominant-ninth harmony; and the return to B major (already noted in the discussion of the continuous sketch in Chapter 4) is achieved with extraordinary skill.

Both the continuous sketch and the first completed version of the Concerto indicate that Dvořák's original intentions in the finale did not include any reference to previous movements. While not all of Dvořák's American works include thematic recall, it was a technique he resorted to fairly frequently while working in the New World. Cyclic features had been appearing in his work from early in his career (we have already noted that the finale of the first Cello Concerto includes material from its first movement, and Dvořák's most comprehensively cyclic work of all is the early E minor String Quartet, B 19, from the late 1860s) and by the middle of the 1870s were an established and successful aspect of his style, as can be seen from the Fifth Symphony (op. 76, B 54) and the Serenades for Strings (op. 22, B 52) and Wind (op. 44, B 77). The overt cyclic impulse retreated temporarily in Dvořák's later symphonic works, but it became a major feature when he went to America and even, in the case of the *Te Deum*, slightly before. Both the *Te Deum* and *The American Flag* rely on a return to their opening material as a final gesture, a practice to which Dvořák returned, somewhat less convincingly, in the *American Suite* for piano (op. 98, B 184; orchestrated version: op. 98b, B 190). The case of the 'New World' Symphony is more complex, since the cyclical process is cumulative through each movement and results in what might be described as a 'free fantasia' on melodies from all four movements in the finale. Whereas Dvořák's use of the procedure in the 'New World' Symphony has often provoked criticism,[32] in the Cello Concerto, the recall of themes from the first and second movements, once noticed – none of the critics at the first performance seems to have done – has been the subject of nothing but warm approval.[33]

In nature the recall of material in the finale's coda is of a different order from his employment of the technique prior to this. It is quite unlike the clinching gestures that crown the conclusions to the two Serenades, nor is it comparable to the summation in the finale of the 'New World' Symphony. The gentleness of the mood surrounding the quotations in the Cello Concerto is reminiscent of the exquisite return of the first movement theme in the finale of the Fifth Symphony – more a reminder than a rounding off gesture. The role of recall as a symbol of memory will be considered in the next chapter, but an examination of its musical presentation and character seems an appropriate conclusion here. Dvořák not only provides an emotionally satisfying close to the

Ex. 5.9(a), (b) and (c)

(a)

(b)   [Allegro moderato]

(c)   [Andante]

work by his use of reminiscences, he also reveals a fundamental family resemblance in his musical material. It is evident that most of the motivic substance in the coda is developed from the opening idea of the finale: in augmentation in the chords at its beginning, and with slight rhythmic alteration (the change of the quaver and two semiquavers in the second bar of the theme to a triplet) in the cello part from bar 425 (see Ex. 5.9a; for the original version of the first theme see Ex. 2.2b). The use of this gentle transformation of the main theme is pervasive throughout the first part of the coda. As any sense of harmonic movement dissolves into a sustained B major, motivic features are broken down into more elemental building blocks (see Ex. 5.9b). Against this background, the use of the opening theme of the first movement, in the clarinets and 'introduced' by the cello (see Ex. 5.9c), seems almost as much a revelation of profound similarity of outline as a significant recall: a recognition of the generative role of the interval of the third in these two movements.

6

The score II: interpretations

A concerto for orchestra?

The Cello Concerto was by no means the only concertante project which Dvořák considered during his stay in America. In the summer and autumn of 1893, he seems to have had thoughts about a violin concerto (possibly also a symphony) in G minor and another concerto without instrumental designation.[1] Even more intriguing was another idea which Dvořák toyed with, also in 1893. According to a note in the first American sketchbook the work in question was to be a: 'Concerto for orchestra, in each movement one of the instruments dominates'.[2] Unfortunately this boldly imaginative project, which anticipates Hindemith, Kodaly and Bartók by several decades, remained unrealised, but the tendency towards an orchestral style in which one instrument dominates had already emerged in the second movement of the 'New World' Symphony, with its extended and unforgettable solo for the cor anglais. From many points of view, the Cello Concerto develops a similar impulse. While no specific solo instrument challenges the dominant position of the cello, it is by no means the only soloist to be featured. Apart from the memorable use of the horn in the first movement there are notable solos for other instruments: the solo flute in the A-flat minor section of the first movement's development (see bars 229–39), a gathering of wind instruments led again by a solo flute at the *quasi Cadenza* in the Adagio, ma non troppo (bars 112–26) and the solo violin in the finale (bars 347–79 and 468–73).

This ready interplay of instruments clearly struck home with the first reviewers of the work; doubtless Dvořák's handling of the orchestra was in part the reason that prompted the critic of *The Musical Times* to refer to the work as 'three orchestral movements with violoncello obbligato'.[3] His rather more perspicacious colleague at *The Times* noted that: 'just balance is maintained between the orchestra and the solo instruments';[4] the use of the plural is significant and shows the clear recognition that more than just the solo cello had a share of the limelight. The views of the critic of *The Musical Times* may also have been conditioned by the size of the orchestra. As we have seen, Dvořák took a lead from Herbert's Second Cello Concerto in using the largest orchestra he had fielded in a concerto hitherto, adding three trombones, a tuba and a piccolo (a triangle is also added in the finale) to the standard line up of double woodwind, horns, trumpets, timpani and strings. Nevertheless, Dvořák was distinctly sparing with the full orchestral tutti, using it strictly to delineate the major formal junctures.[5] A major feature of the orchestration apparent in all three movements is the frequency of a chamber-like quality involving the continual reconfiguring of instrumental combinations, mostly with, though sometimes without, the soloist.

Dvořák's lightness of touch not only affects the handling of the solo cello in such passages as the accompaniment to the second theme in the solo exposition in the first movement (bar 139 ff.), the A-flat minor episode in the same movement's development (bar 223 ff.), much of the slow movement and the G major episode in the finale (bar 281 ff.), but also the way in which other solo instruments are treated, notably the horn's presentation of the second theme in the orchestral exposition of the first movement (bar 56 ff.) and the solo violin's leading of the B major episode in the finale (bar 347 ff.). Along with this deftness in accompaniment is a novel exploration of timbre, chief among which is the use of the timpani. Dvořák might well have taken a lead from his own use of the timpani in the orchestration of the Rondo in G minor for cello and small orchestra where they underpin the solo cello line, marked *ppp*, in the return of the rondo theme at bar 112 ff. In the Cello Concerto, Dvořák employs a similar effect as part of the background to the soloist's playing of the third and fourth main phrases of the second theme in the recapitulation of the first movement (bars 275–80); still more memorable is the way in which the timpani provide a triplet articulation of the bass under the cello's last descent in the coda of the finale (bars 485–93).[6]

Of equal originality is Dvořák's readiness to experiment with combinations of wind instruments and the solo cello without any string support. His debt to Herbert's Second Cello Concerto where brass usage was concerned has already been acknowledged (see Chapter 2), but in his novel treatment of the wind-band he owed nothing to Herbert, who usually made sure the strings provided support if not actual doubling for wind instruments on most occasions where they are prominent. There are examples of this approach to orchestration in Dvořák's Violin Concerto, in particular the accompaniment to the first entry of the soloist in the first movement (bars 5–11), the link to the slow movement (see especially bars 253–8) and, a little more extensively, in the finale, but these have little of the penetrating originality of certain passages in the Cello Concerto. That Dvořák had begun to approach the question of more flexible handling of the woodwind in more recent work is clear from the Eighth Symphony; where concertante compositions were concerned, the use of woodwind in the Rondo in G minor may be unadventurous, but the combination of cello solo and wind instruments in *Silent Woods* (see Chapter 2, Ex. 2.1) certainly prefigures Dvořák's orchestral manner in the Concerto.

In the Cello Concerto the orchestral fabric is frequently reduced to near chamber music combinations involving woodwind and the soloist. One of the more ear-catching – although it involves the orchestral viola line, albeit in a distinctly percussive role – is the end of the *Quasi improvisando* first entry of the cello six bars before the return to Tempo 1 (see Ex. 6.1). Of a similar order is the return of the song quotation 'Lasst mich allein!', from bar 68 of the Adagio, ma non troppo, where the cello provides accompaniment as two pairs of clarinets and bassoons play the theme in thirds while the role of the strings is reduced to a minimal pizzicato outlining of the bass for cellos and double basses. The slow movement's coda (bar 149 ff.) is also a cue for the attention to focus on the woodwind, with only the barest shading from the strings. In the finale, much the same may be said of the second part of the solo exposition (bars 49–56, see Ex. 1.1b), where the lower strings merely articulate the bass while most of the emphasis is thrown on to the combination of wind and solo cello, and the start of the G major episode is given over entirely to the solo cello, bassoons and clarinets (see bars 281–93). The *locus classicus* of this approach to orchestral compartmentalisation, which demands quotation, is the *quasi Cadenza* after the return of the main melody in the slow movement (bars 107–28). This passage has

Ex. 6.1

already been cited for its similarity to part of *Silent Woods*, but what Dvořák offers in the Concerto is of a completely different order. Its rapt, cadenza-like qualities for all the instruments involved – providing, incidentally, considerable problems of co-ordination given the conventional layout of the orchestra – lift it away from the basic orchestral texture: a cadenza, not just for the soloist, but for an ensemble of instruments which, through its clear evocation of bird-song and pervasive sense of pastoral reverie, make it unique in the Romantic concerto repertoire (see Ex. 6.2). The effect of the passage, with its rhythmic freedom and highly ornamental character, inevitably creates a sensational impression, but virtually all of the latter part of the slow movement is an intensification of the tendency felt from the beginning to favour wind combinations over ones involving strings. The return of the main theme is given to the horns with the lower strings providing rhythmic pointing, and throughout the rest of the recapitulation and coda the winds predominate with the strings furnishing hardly more than the faintest shading.

In many ways this free and eminently captivating association of small sections of the wind orchestra with the soloist reinforces the view of the work as primarily orchestral with cello obbligato, in many places a veritable 'concerto for orchestra'; but to accept this definition unquestioningly would be to neglect the craft with which Dvořák both integrates the cello into the orchestra and allows it to assert itself independently of the broader texture. The presentation of the first entry of the soloist in the first movement, *Quasi improvisando*, almost in the manner of a cadenza – comparable to the first movements of his own Violin Concerto and that of Brahms's Double Concerto with its extensive introductory cadenza – is a means of clearing overt display out of the way, of establishing virtuosity without exclusively focusing on it. Texturally, the business of this Concerto is not so much the aggrandisement of the soloist, but an exploration of timbral combinations against a gradually evolving formal and tonal background. The cello is a potent presence, but it is not by any means always centre-stage. A particularly delightful example of the cello as part of the orchestral texture comes in the episode in the first movement's solo exposition, repeated almost exactly in the recapitulation, where the cello offers the lightest, skittering accompaniment to a new woodwind figure (bar 158 ff., see Ex. 6.3).[7]

Ex. 6.2

Ex. 6.3

A similar effect is achieved in the latter part of the G major episode in the finale, when the solo cello gently articulates the background string texture as an accompaniment to the solo flute (bars 315–31). This free flow of textures is not an exercise in orchestral democracy for its own sake. From the start of his international career Dvořák had always been noted for his virtuosity in handling the orchestra; one only need think of the twenty-seven-year-old Elgar's comment to Charles Buck after playing in the first violins in a performance of Dvořák's *Stabat Mater* and Sixth Symphony under the composer's baton at the Worcester Three Choirs Festival of 1884: 'I wish you could hear Dvořák's music. It is simply ravishing, so tuneful and clever and the orchestration is wonderful: no matter how few instruments he uses it never sounds thin. I cannot describe it, it must be heard.'[8] As a whole the Cello Concerto marks a considerable advance on the practice of featuring reduced groupings of instruments which is such a delightful feature of the slow movements of the Eighth and Ninth Symphonies. In the Concerto, however, the practice of focusing on these groupings spreads across the entire work, giving a much broader range of opportunity. The only down side, and it is minimal, is that the proliferation of independent lines can impede movement when the contrapuntal elaboration becomes overly tendentious; the only notable example is in the finale where a canonic duet between solo cello and flute (followed by the same with solo oboe) seems unnecessarily fussy (Ex. 6.4).

Ex. 6.4

An operatic concerto?

The ready tendency among commentators – myself included – to resort to vocal terminology when describing aspects of the Concerto throws the spotlight on to its intensely lyrical aspects. In describing, for example, the second main episode in the finale on its return in B major with its distinctive writing for solo violin and cello, Šourek states that the instruments 'sing a duet of intoxicating beauty and irresistible emotional ardour'.[9] For Robertson, the second subject of the first movement is 'sung' by the solo horn,[10] and in Robert Battey's view the G major episode in the finale is a 'noble song'.[11] While there is no evidence that the Concerto is based on operatic material or follows an operatic plan, as Beckerman argues on behalf of parts of the 'New World' Symphony,[12] its prevailingly lyrical character and the way in which Dvořák prepares for this lyricism quite frequently suggest parallels with opera.

If not actively engaged in composing opera, for much of his creative life Dvořák was considering operatic projects of various kinds. The main operatic fruit of his time in America was a full-scale reworking of his grand opera *Dimitrij* (op. 64, B 127 and B 186), but he was also much preoccupied with the possibility of an opera based on Longfellow's *The Song of Hiawatha*; according to Kovařík: 'During his entire time in America he had Hiawatha on his mind. He was immensely captivated by it, kept talking about it, reflected on it, and worked on it with special love, delicacy, and with a huge interest and fervour.'[13] Although some of this material found its way into the 'New World' Symphony, in the end the opera (or cantata) merely generated a number of tantalising sketches scattered across the first five American sketchbooks. Nevertheless, the impulse to compose an opera remained strong throughout his American stay and seems to have generated a pervasive mythology giving rise to rumours of the existence of an American opera. As late as 1897 intelligence, erroneous as it turned out, reached *The Musical Times* that: 'Antonín Dvořák is said to be engaged upon a new opera on the subject of "Uncle Tom's Cabin" which is to be first brought out in the United States'.[14] While it would be unwise to speculate that the Cello Concerto has any material connection with *The Song of Hiawatha*, still less *Uncle Tom's Cabin*, the fact that opera was still very much in mind is significant. Moreover, after a brief period of reacclimatisation on his return to Bohemia, Dvořák devoted the remainder of his career to a series of five symphonic poems, four of them explicitly programmatic, and the composition of opera.[15] While we have explored the rights and wrongs of the Concerto being a link back to symphonic orthodoxy, if it is to be placed realistically within the broader span of Dvořák's career, as it deserves, it seems appropriate to consider the work as a transition to a part of his creative life in which abstract music did not feature at all and which was dominated almost entirely by opera.

In a concerto for an instrument with the lyrical capacity of the cello, it is perhaps unsurprising to find vocal parallels in Dvořák's writing for it. Šourek was prompted to two direct comparisons with opera in his discussion of the first movement of the Concerto. The first is a parallel between the clarinet counter-melody to the cello's new theme at bar 166 and the second phrase of the hunter's song in the first act of *Rusalka* (see Ex. 6.5a and 6.5b); the second is a much more tenuous connection between the rising horn triplets at bar 176 in the first movement and the theme associated with Přemysl's love for Libuše in Smetana's opera of the same name (the figure dominates his first aria in act II scene 3 of the opera).[16] Such more or less fortuitous resemblances hardly qualify the Concerto for operatic status, but other aspects of Dvořák's treatment of his lyricism might. A number of the transitions have almost the quality of scene changes, or at least changes of atmosphere, in Dvořák's mature

Ex. 6.5(a) and (b)

Ex. 6.6

operas. A notable example is the move from the statement of the main theme in the finale (bars 246–65) to the G major episode. Not only does Dvořák effect a modulation from B minor to G major, but he completely alters the atmosphere from stormy aggression to pastoral contentment within the space of sixteen bars via an extension of the concluding phrase of the main theme crowned by an aspiring oboe solo (see Ex. 6.6). Even more striking is Dvořák's approach to the first appearance of the second theme in the first movement. Although its uniquely lyrical qualities already set it apart from the rest of the movement, Dvořák prepares

Ex. 6.7(a) [Rusalka] and (b)

for it with a string wind-down that finds an almost exact parallel in the second act of *Rusalka* in a passage depicting the onset of twilight just before the arrival of the wedding guests (see Ex. 6.7a and 6.7b). Once again, this transition not only sets the scene for an entirely different order of melody, it also fundamentally changes the mood from the vigorous activity of the first part of the exposition to one of expectant repose.

In addition to this novel approach to transition, there is an infectiously vocal quality to the cello's treatment of a number of the themes. Although the second theme of the first movement does not have an upbeat at its first appearance, it acquires an expressive, expository rising sixth when the cello announces it in the solo exposition and recapitulation. Similarly, the first theme of the Adagio gains a preludial crotchet upbeat as the cello takes up the theme (see Ex. 6.8a and 6.8b). The cello also seems to be fulfilling a quasi-vocal role in the coda of the finale, introducing, like a commentator or Greek chorus, the quotations from the two previous movements. These qualities, so readily typified as vocal or operatic, undoubtedly contribute to the Concerto's uniqueness within Dvořák's output. In the 1880s, when he was at work on a variety of projects including oratorio, symphony, chamber music and, at either end

Ex. 6.8(a) and (b)

(a)   Adagio, ma non troppo

Cl. I

(b)   [Adagio, ma non troppo]

Solo
Cello

of the decade, opera, he seems to have put something of a premium on compartmentalising these various activities; there is little seepage from the dramatic vocal works into the abstract instrumental music, although this was not the case the other way round: the Requiem Mass for Birmingham benefited greatly from an infusion of symphonic fibre. In the 1890s, and particularly when Dvořák was in America, matters were different: Dvořák's various activities, including even unachieved operatic projects, flowed more readily together. While an inability to get to grips with an American opera – two Hiawatha librettos were considered and hopeful press announcements made – is not the sole explanation for the inception of the Cello Concerto, surely it is not too far fetched to speculate that its proto-vocal tendencies might have been fired by a frustration that he was not actively engaged on an operatic project. Before the explicitly programmatic late symphonic poems, with their panoply of speech melodies, the Cello Concerto is the most operatic of Dvořák's orchestral works; not a work in search of a plot, but one that is energised at many fundamental junctures by the techniques and rhetoric of opera. But this is not the only feature to disturb the abstract credentials of the conventional view of the Concerto; another favourite feature apparent in the literature is its nostalgia.

A spiritual homecoming?

Neither Hoffmeister writing in 1924 nor Tovey in 1936 breathes a word about nostalgia or a longing for home in the Concerto. Edwin Evans, on the other hand, in 1942, refers to: 'The nostalgic feeling ascribed to this

Concerto is concentrated in the meditative slow movement, the melodic line of which suggests Dvořák's homeland'.[17] Imprecise as this is, it introduces two related strands which have been taken up by most commentators since. Šourek offers slightly more substance in his life and works of Dvořák, when he stated that the Concerto, 'was not inspired by America, but however grew above all out of an immense artistic longing for Bohemia',[18] a point he seems to elaborate on in his study of the orchestral music: 'the Concerto in its emotional content is nourished by longing for home and by memories of his own country and people'.[19] The interpretation of the Concerto as an expression of nostalgia has been so widely accepted that almost no commentator since has avoided use of the 'n' word, a tendency which reached an apotheosis in the consideration of the Concerto in *Dvořák in America, 1892–1895* entitled 'Thoughts of Home'.[20]

While there is no epistolary sanction from Dvořák concerning the precise nature of his feelings when writing the Concerto, there is a significant juxtaposition of sentiment and enthusiasm in a letter to his friend Alois Göbl (see also Chapter 1, no. 4):

> That we are missing the children terribly you can imagine and that we can hardly wait until the spring when, God grant, we return. Once the holiday and New Year are past, time will fly. . . . I want to show you one episode which I reflected on very greatly, but with which in the end I was satisfied. Every time when I play it I tremble.[21]

After this admission, Dvořák quoted the first three and a half bars of the second theme of the first movement of the Cello Concerto as they appear in the solo horn in D major. For a man noted more for his reticence than for a readiness to impart intimate information, this is a major admission. In the context of the letter, Dvořák seems almost to be offering the melody as an earnest of his longing to return home. Still firmer evidence that Dvořák's mind was running ahead of his body as spring approached is furnished by a letter to Josef Boleška sent slightly over a month after the one to Göbl:

> Now I am finishing the finale of the Cello Concerto. If I could work as free from care as at Vysoká [Dvořák's country home] it would have been ready long ago. But here it isn't possible: on Monday I have things to do at school, on Tuesday I have spare time, other days I am also more or less

busy so that I do not have enough time for my work, and when I do, I am not in the mood etc. In short, it would be best to be sitting in Vysoká; there I have the best recreation and repose – and I am happy. If only I were there again![22]

While Dvořák was certainly preoccupied with thoughts of his return to Bohemia while working on the Concerto, what if any was the effect on the work? To focus on the first movement: might there not be a subtext to the treatment of the first and second subjects and their relationship to the overall structure of the movement – a movement which, as we have already discussed, so clearly challenges convention? The use of the first subject (the determined, 'masculine' element of the movement) at the 'still centre' of the development, robbed of nearly all sense of motion, is at the opposite end of the emotional spectrum from the triumphant return of the second subject which marks the recapitulation. In searching for a programmatic underpinning, or at the least some guide to the expressive content, in a movement that signally avoids the more engine-like qualities of abstract symphonism, might we not construe this episode – so evidently poignant and meditative, so lacking in symphonic direction – as an image of the composer isolated in America? Similarly, might not the recapitulation – perhaps the most gloriously conclusive the composer ever penned, and crowned by a melody that on his own admission made him 'tremble' – be a joyous outburst at the prospect of a final return to his distant home? There is also the question of the extended coda of the finale; even without the quotations (introduced, of course, after Dvořák had returned to Bohemia) this long, barely diluted stretch of tonic chord would seem to suggest the contentment to which Dvořák alluded in his letter to Boleška. To uncover a deeper meaning, however, we must go back in space and time some thirty years to Dvořák's days as a jobbing viola player and music teacher in Prague.

Josefina's concerto?

In 1865 Dvořák fell in love with Josefina Čermáková, the second of five daughters of the Prague goldsmith Jan Čermák. The main authority for this identification of Dvořák's first love is Šourek,[23] though he is supported by the reminiscences of Otakar Dvořák.[24] Dvořák's song cycle *Cypresses* from the summer of the same year was thought to have been prompted by a burgeoning love for his sixteen-year-old music pupil. No intimate relationship came of his affections, if indeed Josefina was particularly aware of them, since he was very shy with women at this stage,[25] but Dvořák's contact with the family continued and in 1873 he married Josefina's younger sister, Anna. The families remained close. The Dvořáks named their first daughter after Josefina (she lived for only three days) and in later years they would spend holidays at the country home, Vysoká, of Count Kaunitz, to whom Josefina was now married. In the mid-1880s Dvořák bought land from Count Kaunitz and had a country retreat built there. No suggestion of scandal has risen from the relatively simple details of this story, but deep affection between Dvořák and Josefina, perhaps amounting to love if not passion, remained. Although the *Cypresses* song cycle was not published in Dvořák's lifetime, it surfaced in many shapes and forms throughout his career,[26] and may have acted as a reminder of early love.

Although there is no evidence of an extensive correspondence between Dvořák and Josefina before the move to New York in 1892, the families remained close and during the composer's stays in America his mother-in-law, Klotilda Čermáková, looked after the four children who stayed behind in Prague. At a time when Dvořák was certainly focused on his return to Bohemia, Josefina's letter of November 26 must have struck with unusual force.[27] Her messages to the Dvořáks hitherto had contained domestic details and news from home quite different in tone from the new letter; it is certainly more direct and would have given the recipient cause for anxiety. Written by Josefina from the Kaunitzes' house in Smíchov, it ends conventionally enough with Christmas greetings to the Dvořáks from her and her husband. The rest of the letter is a catalogue of woes. Josefina is confined to bed (she had heart problems which eventually killed her) and regrets that she was hardly able to see Dvořák or his wife, her sister Anna, during their summer break in Bohemia, nor attend his farewell concert.[28] She is too unwell to visit Vienna and her husband is out of sorts and often away. Her mother, presumably too busy caring for Dvořák's and Anna's children as well as looking after her lodgers, visits rarely. The whole is a sorry story crowned by Josefina's comment that she might never be 'able to look forward to anything any more'.[29]

Dvořák's immediate practical response to this doleful news was a letter to his mother-in-law and his children that remained in Prague. In it he says that he hopes for Josefina's health (he refers to her by the familiar diminutive 'Pepinka'), also that they are concerned his mother-in-law is overworking and that they will readily pay for the hire of a maid. The letter is dated 7 December 1894 and seems to be a firm indication that they had already received Josefina's 26 November communication by this time.[30] Another letter, dated 11 December 1894, and again sent to his mother-in-law and the children, mentions that he had written to 'Auntie Pepi', but unfortunately the letter does not appear to have survived.[31] Further letters to his family dated 11 and 25 January 1895 state that he would be writing to her, but again nothing remains. Nevertheless, the relative frequency of these letters home and the somewhat nervous references to Josefina indicate a strong level of alarm.

The musical result of the letter is indicated by the appearance of the song and its role in the composition of the slow movement of the Concerto. Once again we have to rely on Šourek for the fact that 'Lasst mich allein!' was a favourite of Josefina.[32] Even if the song had not been a particular favourite of hers, it could hardly be bettered as a personal response from the composer to the sorry circumstances in which she languished. Not only does the melody of the second verse have a pungently bitter-sweet quality, with harmony hovering between major and minor, the words must also have seemed significant. At one time Dvořák might have reflected, with a certain ruefulness, that the title of the song could have been the words she once used to him; now their resonance registers alarm at her sorry state as much as acting as a reminder of how he once felt for her: 'Leave me alone! Do not banish with your noisy words the peace in my breast.'[33] The general tenor of the poem – one of four set by Dvořák as his op. 82 and which Šourek dismissed as: 'not rising above mediocre sentimental-erotic versification'[34] – has something of the mawkish sense of longing of Chamisso's verse used by Schumann in *Frauenliebe und -leben*. Dvořák's setting, however, has a breadth and melodic flexibility which lifts the sentiment of the poem far above the triteness of its verse. Similarly, his treatment of the song in the central section of the slow movement of the Concerto constitutes some of the most expressive writing in the whole work.

At its first appearance the melody is enunciated by the solo cello and accompanied lightly by strings and a counter-melody for the clarinet; a brief comparison with the vocal line of the song will show the extent to

Ex. 6.9(a) and (b)

(a) [Andante]

(b) [Adagio, ma non troppo]

which Dvořák has altered the melody, including the addition of a new tail-piece (Ex. 6.9a and 6.9b). Having established the identity of the theme, however, Dvořák's elaborations take on increasingly expressive qualities. As the flute and oboe take over with a variant of the melody, the solo cello adds a chromatic sigh to the falling nature of the line to exquisite effect (see Ex. 6.10). Later, after a repeat of the introductory G minor outburst, as clarinets and bassoons in pairs take up the theme, harmonised in thirds, the solo cello dances attention on the melody with filigree figuration (bars 69–75). Once stated, the wistful tone of the song casts a

Ex. 6.10

shadow over the open-hearted melody of the beginning of the movement: the return of the main theme, played in close harmony on the
horns, is underpinned with elegiac, funeral-march judders in the lower
strings (bars 95–107).

While undoubtedly effective on its own terms, the frank symbolism of
the funeral march in the recapitulation must have seemed strangely pro-
phetic when, on 27 May 1895, Josefina died. As if to confirm the personal
significance of the Concerto, Dvořák's response was to add reminiscences
from the first and second movements to the coda in an extensive reworking of the very end of the Concerto. In refashioning the conclusion of the
work he may have had in mind a model which lay at the very heart of the
Czech tradition, Smetana's First String Quartet in E minor; the work was
well known to Dvořák since he had played the viola in its first, private performance in the home of the writer Josef Srb-Debrnov in April 1878. Not
only is there a parallel in the autobiographical content of the two works –
much more extensive, of course, in Smetana's quartet – the mechanics by
which they are externalised in the finales have considerable similarities.
In both works, the finale, an apparently cheerful rush to the double bar, is
interrupted by an extended coda: in Smetana's quartet the abrupt curtail-
ing of the peroration and the subsequent reminiscence of earlier melodies
were intended to shock; though similar in ethos and outline, Dvořák's
coda – while it halts the celebratory nature of the conclusion led by the
solo cello – has none of the angst of Smetana's ending. Harmonic movement and texture are broadened out for more leisured reflection. Tovey,
in speaking of the slow movement and finale, states that both 'relapse into

Ex. 6.11

Ex. 6.12

Charles the Second's apologies for being such an unconscionable time in dying'.[35] The sentiment if not the emphasis could well be right; the finale is, indeed, a long good-bye. With hindsight concerning Dvořák's feelings and ultimately his sadness on the death of his first love, the musings of the cello take on a more poignant significance. After its initial fall from a pedal B (bars 437–53, all part of the coda with which Dvořák had concluded the Concerto's finale in America), the solo cello pursues an ascending line, almost like a mind rising through levels of consciousness, to introduce the first theme of the first movement (see Ex. 5.9c) and then, exquisitely shaded by a solo violin, Josefina's song (Ex. 6.11). Following this, Dvořák unites the themes as the cello falls (see Ex. 6.12). Our last hearing of the two themes is only bars before the Andante maestoso, molto accelerando and Allegro vivo which conclude the Concerto. The solo cello plays the falling element of Josefina's theme while the rising third of the opening theme of the first movement is repeated in the orchestral violins over alternating, sweetly dissonant harmonies (Ex. 6.12, bar 4). While musically satisfying, to suggest that this passage, so clearly laden with

Ex. 6.13(a) and (b)

(a)   Adagio quasi Largo

(b)   [Allegro moderato]
        [Meno mosso]

meaning, is merely the fortuitous outcome of an improvisatory combination of themes is too bland. The uniting of these two thematic elements is seductively evocative of what might have been in Dvořák's life if his love for Josefina had had a chance to flower.

The tissue of allusion in these final bars has been charmingly extended by Jitka Slavíková[36] who sees in the solo cello's fall from its highest note (two octaves above middle C) an echo of the final duet of Tatiana and Onegin in Tchaikovsky's *Eugene Onegin* at the point at which Tatiana, followed by Onegin, sings the words: 'Happiness was so close at hand' (Ex. 6.13a, cf. Ex. 6.13b). The melodic resemblance is certainly there, though Tchaikovsky's harmony is a dominant seventh set as an appoggiatura over a tonic pedal, followed by a tonic close, while Dvořák's is cast over a long minor seventh on the subdominant resolving, after the melodic sentence is over, on to the tonic. Dvořák knew *Eugene Onegin* well and admired it;[37] in this context, moreover, the words are certainly significant. Within the confines of Dvořák's own work, there may also be a further allusion back to the songs he is purported to have written for Josefina, *Cypresses* of 1865. Clapham has pointed out the resemblance between the falling nature of the melody of 'Lasst mich allein!' and 'Zde v lese' ('Here in the forest'),[38] the fourteenth of the *Cypresses* collection. It is interesting to note that when Dvořák revised

Ex. 6.14(a) and (b)

the song as the sixth of the eight *Love Songs* (op. 83, B 160), he transferred the piano's falling accompanying line of 1865 to the voice (see Ex. 6.14a and 6.14b and cf. with Ex. 6.11 above). Once again the poetry tempts an interpretation pertinent to the emotional significance of the end of the Concerto: 'Here in the forest by a stream I stand all alone and into the waves I gaze in thought. Here I see an old stone over which the waves foam; that stone rises, falls unceasingly under the waves. And on it the current bears down until the stone dissolves; when will the wave of life carry me from the world?'[39] A final intimation of mortality is to be found in Casals' interpretation of the flattening of the major third in the solo cello line in bar 8 of Ex. 6.12 (see *x*). According to David Blum, Casals – who would tell a student about to embark on the first solo entry in the first movement: 'Announce the hero!' – saw this as a 'moment of final expiration . . . portraying "the death of the hero"'.[40] Dvořák himself referred to the finale's gradual close as a 'diminuendo like a sigh – with reminiscences from the first and second movements'.[41] In the same letter to Simrock, Dvořák went on to say that 'the last bars are taken up by the orchestra and [the movement] closes in stormy mood'. The sigh ['Hauch'] to which Dvořák refers may indeed be one of expiration, but in the stillness after the resolution on to the tonic at bar 493, with its curious pair of chords (D major followed by G major on a dominant pedal in B major), the sigh might as easily be that of a lover's final farewell before turning back to the world.

To argue for a complex system of ciphers in Dvořák's output, focused on this Concerto, would be over-ambitious. But in the work of a composer who kept his personal emotions well hidden, the unusual circumstance of an aspect of his psyche coming so evidently to the surface demands recognition. In the case of the Cello Concerto, interpretative investigation yields some remarkably coherent results. If the hermeneutics of these glosses on the coda of the finale seem slightly tortured, they are, nevertheless, an understandable response to an extended moment whose numinous qualities communicate even without recourse to a detailed explanation. In teasing out the explanation, a dimension of astonishing humanity emerges in the work of a composer who is, all too often, dismissed as unreflective.[42]

Performers and performances

Wihan and virtuosity

By the time the thirty-three-year-old Wihan succeeded his teacher František Hegenbarth as professor of cello at the Prague Conservatory in 1888, he was already a seasoned performer. He had been appointed a professor at the Mozarteum in Salzburg at the tender age of eighteen and had played in orchestras in Berlin, Sonderhausen and Munich. During his time as principal cellist of the Court Orchestra at Munich, Wihan became acquainted with Richard Strauss, gave a number of performances of the young composer's early Romance for cello and orchestra, and took part in the première of his String Quartet in A major, op. 2, on 14 March 1881. Strauss, for his part, dedicated his Cello Sonata, op. 6, 'Seinem lieben Freunde Herrn Hans Wihan' and then promptly fell passionately in love with Wihan's wife, Dora.[1]

The part he played in convincing Dvořák that the cello was a suitable concertante instrument and his prompting of the composer to write the Concerto has already been rehearsed. But his role did not stop with inspiration. Dvořák was certainly willing to take advice from cellists while composing the work. One such was the Dutch cellist Josef Hollmann (1852–1927) about whose reaction to the Concerto Dvořák wrote as follows:

> The Concerto for Cello will soon be ready [the letter was written on 28 January 1894 in New York only days before he first completed the Concerto on 9 February], I have only the finale to complete. There is here an excellent cellist, Hollmann from London; he was with me and I played him the Concerto; he both liked it and congratulated me that it was very successful.[2]

Ex. 7.1

Wihan's advice came to the fore in September 1895. On a visit to the mansion of Josef Hlávka (founder of the Czech Academy of Arts and Sciences and a confidant of Dvořák) at Lužany with members of the Czech (Bohemian) Quartet, which he had founded in 1891, Wihan played through the Concerto with the composer at the piano. Dvořák wanted him to supply fingerings and bowing; in addition, Wihan suggested a number of significant changes to the solo part in the first and second movements, some of which Dvořák saw the benefit of and accepted.[3] One of the most striking of Wihan's suggestions concerned the cello solo accompaniment in the transition section in the solo exposition of the first movement (bars 158–65). Dvořák's original intentions had been a workmanlike, but rather dull, semiquaver oscillation based on a figure in the previous bar (Ex. 7.1, version 1);[4] he then moved towards a fussier form of semiquaver figuration (Ex. 7.1, version 2) which in many ways was even less satisfactory. Wihan seems to have persuaded him to adopt the much bolder figure based on falling and rising semiquaver triplets (see Ex. 6.3) on which he finally settled. Though far more dashing than Dvořák's earthbound first thought, it creates formidable problems of intonation for the soloist, as Casals' pioneering recording of 1937 shows.[5] Dvořák's first thought for the F-sharp major melody that emerges at bar 166 in the first movement was originally an extension of the semiquaver oscillations from the previous episode which underpinned the clarinet line. Wihan's suggestion for this passage would have

Ex. 7.2

made the cello line a good deal more sonorous, but was ultimately rejected by Dvořák in favour of a more genuinely lyrical alternative (cf. Ex. 7.2, Dvořák first version; 7.2, Wihan; 7.2, Dvořák final version).

Wihan also seems to have been involved in helping Dvořák crystallise the technically imaginative start of the *quasi Cadenza* starting at bar 107 in the slow movement. The earliest stage of the composer's working manuscript of the score indicates that Dvořák had considered chording of some kind, but neither of his initial attempts (see Ex. 7.3a and 7.3b) include the inspired idea of adding pizzicato in the bass (see Ex. 6.2). Later in this passage, Wihan seems to have helped by simplifying the figuration under the solo flute's descending arpeggios and trills (slow movement, bar 117, see Ex. 6.2, bar 11). Dvořák's first thoughts, involving the complex arpeggio figures he adopted in bar 118, would certainly have interfered with the flute line. The chords for which he opted, presumably prompted by Wihan, are, musically speaking, far more satisfactory. They, pose, however, a peculiarly tortuous, and virtually insurmountable, technical problem in that both the upper notes of the chord cannot be sustained while still having open strings available for the pizzicato notes.[6]

Ex. 7.3(a) and (b)

This sonority-led approach to technical questions lifts Dvořák's Concerto into a different category from the virtuoso concertante works of the contemporary repertoire. In concertos by the likes of Davïdov, Popper and Herbert, the nature of the virtuosity, while fearsome, is designed to dazzle; Dvořák's intentions, as we saw in the previous chapter, are focused much more on the expansion of timbre and the interaction between the cello and other instruments; the illuminating paradox is that the point at which he includes a passage that is virtually unplayable, as in the *quasi Cadenza* of the slow movement, is a moment of quiet reflection rather than extrovert display. This antithesis of the conventional role of virtuosity in the Concerto perhaps explains the reaction of the critic of *The Musical Times* to the first performance: 'Concertos for [the soloist] Mr Stern's instrument should be written, if possible, by the performers, who would take good care to make the *soli* effective and see the orchestra kept back in its place. Not being a *virtuoso*, and not bearing sufficiently in mind the fact that the violoncello does not "carry" well, Dvořák has written *soli* which are a good deal covered up, as well as eclipsed in interest by the orchestral music.'[7]

The same critic's response perhaps also reflects the absence of any celebration of virtuosity in a solo cadenza. While Dvořák and Wihan seem to have been in harmony regarding many aspects of the work, the cellist's desire for a cadenza did not meet with the composer's approval at all. The fifty-nine-bar cadenza which Wihan supplied[8] is conscientious in its use of material from the Concerto. The beginning and end of this effusion make use of the opening theme of the first movement, a move that was probably prompted by the point in the finale where he intended

89

to insert the cadenza (bar 461), just where Dvořák introduces a reminiscence of the theme. The middle section returns – perhaps with proprietary chutzpah, given his role in firming up the cello line – to the *quasi Cadenza* of the slow movement (bars 107–19). For all Wihan's good intentions, and he probably didn't know anything about the intensely emotional background to the work, the placing of the cadenza in the midst of Dvořák's carefully structured tissue of allusions to earlier parts of the Concerto and his externalising of virtuosity for its own sake were crass and fundamentally at odds with the ethos of the work. Dvořák's reaction, enshrined in a letter to his publisher Simrock, dated 3 October 1895, was devastatingly direct:

> With friend Wihan I have had disagreements over *certain places*. Some of these passages don't please me – and I must insist that my work is published as I wrote it. These particular passages can be printed in two ways, the *easier* and *harder* manner.[9] I shall only give you the work if you promise that *no one*, including my respected friend Wihan, makes *alterations without my knowledge* and *consent*; also not [i.e. do not print] the cadenza which Wihan has put into the last movement – it must stay in its original form, as I felt and imagined it. The cadenza in the last movement is neither in the score nor the piano arrangement. I told Wihan straight away when he showed it to me, that it is impossible to stick a bit like this on. The finale closes gradually diminuendo like a sigh – with reminiscences from the first and second movements – the solo dies down to *pp* and then swells again, and the last bars are taken up by the orchestra and it finishes in stormy mood.
>
> That was my idea and from it I cannot depart.[10]

Leo Stern and the première

Given the importance of his role in many aspects of the creation of the Cello Concerto, there is a huge irony in the fact that Wihan did not give the first performance. Despite Dvořák's annoyance with Wihan's cadenza, his exclusion from the première came about as a result of practical, rather than personal, reasons. Dvořák fully intended Wihan to give the first performance at a Philharmonic Society concert in London with himself conducting. Wihan was agreeable to their terms, but could not manage the suggested date of 19 March 1896, instead favouring an alternative in April. The Philharmonic Society went ahead with 19 March, however, and to Dvořák's amazement informed him, as late as February, that Stern had been engaged. Dvořák – who had suggested Wihan for the première in a letter to Francesco Berger, the secretary of the Philharmonic Society, dated 13 November 1895, and wrote again at Christmas to say that the cellist could not manage 19 March – was clearly surprised and dismayed. His response to Berger's announcement that the concert was going ahead on 19 March seems a reasonable indication that he fully intended Wihan to première the Concerto under his direction:

> I am sorry to announce you that I cannot conduct the performance of the Cello Concerto [celo conzerto]. The reason is I have promised to my friend Wihan – *he will play it*.
>
> If you put the Concerto into the program, I could not come at all, and will be glad to come another time.[11]

Berger wrote four days later saying that they would remove the Concerto from the programme.[12] Between Berger's reply and Dvořák's next surviving letter to him, dated 2 March, no correspondence between them survives, though the problem concerning Wihan and the première had clearly been surmounted. Dvořák's letter already speaks about rehearsals and says that Stern likes the Concerto;[13] he wrote again the next day stating that: 'Mr Stern plays every day with me and I hope he will be all right'.[14] Like Wihan, Stern had received tuition from Davïdov. The circumstances of his first meeting with the composer are unknown, but he toured extensively in Europe with the singer Emma Albani, who had worked with Dvořák. Certainly, in the three weeks leading up to the première both the composer and performer were evidently close.

The first performance seems to have been a considerable success, despite some less than entirely favourable circumstances, as *The Times* noted:

> By an unfortunate arrangement two of the most interesting and important concerts of the present season took place last night. As the dates of the Philharmonic concerts were not announced until some months after those of the London Symphony concerts had been fixed and published, a good many members of the Philharmonic orchestra were represented last night by deputies, and the material was not quite as fine as usual. Nevertheless, the result obtained from the players by Herr Dvořák, of whose compositions the programme mainly consisted, was almost irreproachable, and quite unusual regard was paid to light and shade.[15]

So 'irreproachable' in fact that the Concerto made an almost entirely favourable impression on the critic, as did Stern's playing:

> In wealth and beauty of thematic material, as well as in the unusual interest of the development of its first movement, the new Concerto yields to none of the composer's recent works; all three movements are richly melodious, the just balance is maintained between the orchestra and the solo instruments, and the passages written for display are admirably devised. . . . Mr Leo Stern played the solo part with good taste, musicianly expression, and faultless technical skill, and the work was received with much enthusiasm.

The critic of the *Musical Courier* concurred, noting that Stern played the solo part 'with much expression and faultless intonation'.[16] As we have already noted, the critic of *The Musical Times* was less than convinced by the credentials of the work as a virtuoso concerto, but was prepared to admit that 'Mr Stern discharged an arduous task with success which was as conspicuous as circumstances allowed'.[17] The critic of *The Musical News* was more explicit about the question of balance, noting that: 'Indeed, in many places, the solo was quite obscured by the elaboration of the orchestral parts'.[18] A similar view was held by the critic of *The Athenaeum*, though he is inclined to throw the emphasis on a soloist who played his part 'delicately, though not powerfully'.[19] Dvořák himself seems to have had no doubts about the success of the performance. During the rehearsals he wrote to Jindřich Gesler saying that: 'the orchestra is good and Mr soloist Stern plays very nicely'.[20] Three weeks later Dvořák wrote to Göbl in apparently fulsome terms regarding the première: 'The Cello Concerto was enormously liked and Mr Stern, who yesterday gave the very Concerto here in Prague [the first Prague performance of the Concerto, 11 April 1896, with Dvořák conducting the newly founded Czech Philharmonic], played my piece to my complete satisfaction'.[21] A slightly less positive note then creeps in, suggesting that not everything went entirely swimmingly: 'perhaps here and there one might want it a little different, but one cannot pick and choose and thus must be content to have found someone who could play this Concerto. Were you to have the whole story told of Mr Stern, several sheets of paper would not suffice.'

The slightly mixed views regarding Stern's première of the Concerto could relate as much to the novelty of the work as to the quality of the performance. Unfortunately, there are no recordings of the playing of

Stern, who died at the age of only forty-two in 1904. Dvořák's slight quibbles about his performance probably are a reasonable indication that he would have been happier working with Wihan, though, ironically, he never gave the work with Wihan. The first performances by a Czech cellist were given by Wihan's pupil Artur Krása (1868–1929), first with piano accompaniment in Plzen on 30 May 1896 and Pacov on 7 November, and then with full orchestra in Leipzig on 9 November. At much the same time, the Concerto was beginning to make its way in the wider world. Hugo Becker, who like Stern had studied with Piatti, gave his first performance of the Concerto in Würzburg on 21 October 1896, and was followed by Robert Hausmann in Berlin on 13 November the same year. Julius Klengel, who played the work over with Dvořák in September 1896, gave his first performance in Jena on 23 November. Stern went on to give performances of the Concerto with Nikisch in Leipzig on 3 December 1896 and with Manns in London on 12 December. Meanwhile, the first performance in the United States was given by the American Franz Listemann in New York on 6 December 1896, followed rapidly by Alwin Schroeder in Boston on 18 and 19 December. Thus the performance tradition of the Concerto was relatively well established by the time Wihan got round to his first performance of the Concerto, with Mengelberg and the Concertgebouw in the Hague on 25 January 1899.[22]

The Concerto and Casals

Although the Concerto was taken up relatively readily by the chief virtuosi of the day in Central Europe and America in the years immediately after its composition, by 1943 Alec Robertson reflected that 'It is surprising that we hear this masterly and beautiful work so seldom'.[23] He then added by way of explanation: 'Perhaps our soloists fear to challenge the superb performance of Casals, which is happily perpetuated in the recording made by him'. Casals' version of the Concerto, still viewed as one of the landmarks of recording in the twentieth century, was made at the instigation of Fred Gaisberg, head of artistic policy at EMI, who had worked with the great cellist many times before. The recording, on twelve 78 rpm records, was made with George Szell and the Czech Philharmonic the day after their concert performance in Prague. Both Casals and Szell were enormously satisfied with the result.

Table 7.1

Movement	Casals/ Szell (1937)	Gendron/ Mengelberg (1944)	Navarra/ Stupka (1951)	Fournier/ Szell (1962)
1	13.22	13.54	13.48	14.38
2	10.22	10.35	10.32	11.22
3	11.32	11.40	10.32	12.14
Total:	35.16	36.09	34.52	38.14

Casals' relationship with the Concerto went back nearly to the beginning of the century. He had played it at his debut in Moscow in 1906, apparently to extraordinary effect.[24] His passionate regard for the Concerto was tested to its limits in Paris shortly before the First World War, when he refused to play it under Gabriel Pierné who, just before the concert, disparaged the work. Debussy, who was present, did not support Casals and earned the contempt of the great cellist, who was later to fight a lawsuit for abandoning the concert.[25] His recorded performance is remarkable from many points of view, not least for its approach to tempo. Both Szell and Casals stay very close to the basic metronome indication of $\, = 116$ in the first movement; their tempo in the Adagio, ma non troppo is slightly slower than Dvořák's $\, = 108$, and slightly faster than his $\, = 104$ in the finale (by contrast, his reading of the coda, which is for much of its length $\, = 76$, is slightly slower than the marking). If Casals' and Szell's 1937 performance is viewed as something of a 'gold standard' as far as approaches to tempo are concerned, a glance at important performances over the next two decades reveals strikingly little variation. Maurice Gendron with Mengelberg is, overall, slightly slower than Casals/Szell; Navarra/Stupka are slightly faster (this performance, with the Prague Radio Symphony Orchestra, begins well below Dvořák's metronome mark, but Stupka inserts an *accelerando* which greatly increases the speed leading to the arrival of the full orchestral tutti). By the early 1960s, with Fournier and Szell, the tempi in all three movements seem to have begun to broaden out (see Table 7.1).

The two recorded performances of Casals' younger contemporary Emanuel Feuermann reveal a slightly different picture. Feuermann, who studied with Klengel, who in turn had played the Concerto through with Dvořák, took great interest in Casals' recording (he certainly admired the older cellist, at one point stating that through him 'the cello was established as the fully fledged worthy member of the family of solo instruments'[26]). His first recording was made in 1928 (Allegro; Adagio, ma non troppo) and 1929 (Allegro moderato) and is almost certainly the fastest in existence (1: 11.56; 2: 10.22; 3: 10.30; total: 32.48), mainly by dint of a much higher number of crotchets to the minute than Dvořák recommends in the first movement. The most remarkable aspect of Feuermann's performance, however, is not that he can play it at that speed, but that he plays it so extraordinarily well. His intonation is extremely accurate and the tone throughout has an astonishing sweetness; passages such as the second subject and the A-flat minor episode in the development are relaxed without any sense of haste, despite being played a great deal faster even than Casals. His second recording was made during a concert in New York in 1940 and the tempi are all slower (1: 12.54; 2: 11.39; 3: 10.22; total: 34.55). The reason that, overall, the timing comes in at slightly more than Navarra's 1951 performance is because of a slower tempo adopted in the Adagio, ma non troppo. The tempi for the first movement remain faster than any others apart from his own, but are, nevertheless, only very slightly more than the metronome mark; the performance, once again, is peerless and it is only a matter of regret that recording quality and accompaniment in both his recordings do not reach a higher standard. This crude comparison of metronome markings leaves little room for the role of expressive nuance, but what it can demonstrate is that entirely satisfying performances, such as those of Casals and Feuermann, can and did take place at and around the tempi Dvořák prescribed.

The care and level of respect Casals held for the composer's apparent intentions where tempo and tempo relationships are concerned are enshrined in his own comments about the work. Casals' hermeneutic approach to the Concerto, in which the first subject is seen as the announcement of the hero, has already been touched upon. His approach to the musical architecture was no less thoughtful or involved. Concerning the lead up to the second subject in the solo exposition of the first movement (bars 132 ff., see Ex. 5.4), Casals stated that, 'The whole passage is too long if we make a ritardando', adding 'a diminuendo is

Table 7.2

Bars	1–56 (first subject etc.)	$\quad\quad$ $\,\!= 116$
	57–74 (second subject)	Un poco sostenuto, in tempo
	75–86	Tempo 1, $\,\!= 116$
	87–109 (solo entry)	Quasi improvisando
	110–39	Tempo 1, $\,\!= 116$
	140–57 (second subject)	In tempo, $\,\!= 100$
	158–91 (episode)	Tempo 1, $\,\!= 116$
	192–223 (transition and dev.)	Grandioso
	224–39 (development)	Molto sostenuto, in tempo
		$\,\!= 100$ (still centre)
	240–70	Animato (this section includes the point of recapitulation at bar 267)
	271–84 (recapitulation)	$\,\!= 100$ (second subject)
	285–318	Tempo 1, $\,\!= 116$
	319–28 (Coda)	In tempo, grandioso
	329–41	Più mosso, $\,\!= 132$
	342–54	Tempo 1 grandioso, $\,\!= 116$

enough'.[27] Even where Dvořák indicates a *ritardando* in the slow movement (bar 124) Casals was of the opinion that the tempo should not be retarded too much. The same moderate approach is apparent in his attitude to tempo relationships in all three movements. His view in the first movement was that the second theme should be played only slightly more broadly than the basic tempo, and was against turning the A-flat minor passage in the development into a lento; a clear crotchet pulse was desirable in the slow movement and the G major episode in the finale should not be sentimentalised, though in the coda more freedom was desirable.[28] These common-sense maxims at first sight seem to court banality, and yet they come very close to what Dvořák seems to be trying to indicate in his own tempo instruction in the first movement. Table 7.2 gives an outline of tempo relationships in the first movement.

The movement is unusually rich in points where the basic tempo is flagged up by reference to a metronome mark, as if Dvořák were keen to remind the performer of the main pace after passages at a more relaxed tempo.[29] It is also important to note that both the second subject in the solo exposition and recapitulation have the same metronome marks as

Table 7.3

Movement	Rostropovich/ Karajan (1968)	Rostropovich/ Giulini (1977)	Tortelier/ Previn (1977)
1	15.33	16.23	15.13
2	12.37	12.53	11.30
3	12.53	13.37	12.12
Total:	41.03	42.53	38.55
	Harrell/ Ashkenazy (1982)	Kliegel/ Halász (1991)	Ma/ Masur (1995)
1	15.30	16.06	14.59
2	13.24	12.22	12.31
3	12.56	13.33	12.45
Total:	41.50	42.01	40.15

the A-flat minor section in the development (i.e. $\text{♩} = 100$). And, further-more, Dvořák's intention that the recapitulation should be in the original tempo is confirmed by the lowering of the metronome mark to $\text{♩} = 100$ for the solo cello's playing of the theme *after* the orchestral tutti. In basic ethos, this approach, which seems to be centred on a need to keep the movement going, is reflected by Casals (who plays close to the $\text{♩} = 100$ tempo in both the cited passages) in theory and practice. Common prac-tice in recent decades, however, seems to favour a different view.

The Concerto in the last thirty years

As Fournier's 1962 recording indicates, the scale of performances of the Concerto was beginning to expand away from that which Dvořák seems to have intended. The process has continued in the last thirty years, with playing times regularly in excess of forty minutes. Table 7.3 details a number of recorded performances from the last three decades.

Of the six performances, only Tortelier and Previn are under forty minutes, with Rostropovich and Giulini the slowest. Apart from the broadening out of the tempo in the Adagio, ma non troppo, the second subject and central A-flat minor episode in the first movement and the main part of the Coda in the finale are substantially slower in all cases than the metronome marking. Indeed, in some cases the A–flat minor episode in the first movement's development has become virtually an autonomous miniature slow movement. Another place where approaches have fundamentally altered is in the lead up to the recapitulation in the first movement: Dvořák had no *ritardando* and the chromatic scale leading up to the moment of recapitulation (see Ex. 5.2), though slurred, is not indicated to be played as a slide. Casals and Feuermann are again much closer to what seems to be the composer's intention, with little slowing up in the passage approaching the moment of recapitulation and a fairly straight *a tempo* reading of the chord and rising scale. The practice developed in the last thirty years has been to introduce a general *ritardando*, extend the chord before the recapitulation to a minim (often followed by a beat's rest) and then to turn the rising scale into a roller-coaster slide.

The purpose of this brief examination of performance practice is not to excoriate the inflationary tendencies of performances in the last thirty years. There are, of course, enormous virtues in all of the recordings cited above, not least Rostropovich's wonderfully poetic reading of 1969. But as the Concerto has passed into the continuum it has certainly grown bigger than Dvořák imagined and perhaps intended. Knowledge of the composer's homesickness and the work's connection with Josefina have, perhaps, begun to condition approaches to the work.[30] As it prepares to begin life in the new millennium, it would be a pity if the clarity of line in the work were subverted by too great an emphasis on its sentimental history.

Notes

1 Dvořák and the cello

1 Ludmila Vojáčková-Wechte, 'Antonín Dvořák in the Class Room', *The Etude* 37 (March 1919), p. 135 [hereafter Vojáčková-Wechte].

2 *Ibid.*

3 Josef Michl, 'Z Dvořákova vyprávění', *Hudební revue* 7 (1913–14), p. 402.

4 Milan Kuna, ed., *Antonín Dvořák: korespondence a dokumenty* [*Antonín Dvořák: Correspondence and Documents*], complete edition of letters and documents, vol. III: *1890–1895* (Prague, 1989), p. 329 [all translations unless otherwise indicated are mine] [hereafter Kuna 1989].

5 An exception was the song cycle *Cypresses* [*Cypřiše*]: twelve of the original eighteen songs were published in much revised forms as op. 2 (B 123 and B 124) and op. 83 (B 160).

6 It did in fact turn up, unknown to Dvořák, during his lifetime: a certain Professor Rudolf Dvořák, no relation, bought the manuscript in 1882 from a second-hand dealer in Leipzig, but its existence was not brought to public attention until 1923.

7 'Komposice, které jsem roztrhal a spálil.' Printed in Jarmil Burghauser, *Antonín Dvořák, thematický katalog* [*Antonín Dvořák, Thematic Catalogue*] (Prague, 1996), p. 768 [hereafter Burghauser].

8 See Burghauser, pp. 768–73.

9 For further details about the composition of *Alfred* see Jan Smaczny, '*Alfred*: Dvořák's First Operatic Endeavour Surveyed', *Journal of the Royal Musical Association* 115 (1990), pp. 80–106.

10 The manuscript was eventually acquired by the British Museum. Its première was given on 26 April 1929. Günther Raphael produced an edition that was published by Breitkopf & Härtel in the year of the first performance; his version was a travesty of the original with many cuts and unidiomatic alterations. A reliable version was published in the Dvořák complete edition, vol. IV no. 2. A sensitive and extremely idiomatic orchestration by Jarmil Burghauser was also produced for the complete edition in 1977, vol. VII.

11 Apart from his work in the Provisional Theatre, Dvořák took part in 1878 in the private first performance of Smetana's First String Quartet 'From My Life'.

12 Otakar Šourek, *Život a dílo Antonína Dvořáka* [*Life and Works of Antonín Dvořák*], 3rd edn, vol. III (Prague, 1956), p. 120 [hereafter Šourek 1956].

13 Although Šourek maintained that the part was in the possession of Dvořák's heirs in 1951, it could not be found during the researches associated with the first edition of Burghauser's thematic catalogue, nor was it among the manuscripts transferred to the Czechoslovak State in 1983. See Burghauser, pp. 73–4.

2 Preludes to the Concerto

1 See Kuna 1989, pp. 195–9.

2 See *ibid*, pp. 209–11.

3 The dedication is reproduced in Burghauser, p. 305. Though the Sonatina was dedicated to all his children, it was intended to be played by Otilie (Otilka), piano, and Antonín (Toník), violin.

4 The sketches are preserved in the so-called third American sketchbook (Museum of Czech Music MČH 1675, pp. 17r and 17v); see Burghauser, p. 353, where it is given the catalogue number 419.

5 Dvořák gave the day on which the sketch was made as '10' but left out the month. July is suggested by Burghauser, but June is also possible. The sketch would have coincided with the completion of the continuous sketches for the 'American' Quartet (op. 96, B 179) since it follows on immediately after, though the ink is slightly lighter; also, part of the sketch anticipates material used in the E-flat String Quintet (op. 97, B 180) which Dvořák did not begin to compose until 26 June.

6 John Clapham, 'Dvořák's Cello Concerto in B minor: A Masterpiece in the Making', *Music Review* 40 (1979), pp. 123–40 [hereafter Clapham 1979]. The sketch is in the fifth American sketchbook, pp. 1–22 (Museum of Czech Music MČH 1677); see Burghauser, p. 318.

7 The concert on the evening of Saturday 10 March was preceded by a public rehearsal on the afternoon of 9 March.

8 Reprinted in Edward N. Waters, *Victor Herbert: A Life in Music* (New York, 1955) [hereafter Waters], pp. 87–8.

9 *Ibid*., p. 88.

10 Josef J. Kovařík (1870–1951) was an American-born violinist of Czech ancestry. Born in the Czech-speaking community at Spillville in Iowa, he studied violin at the Prague Conservatory from 1888 to 1891. With his

knowledge of America and ability to speak both Czech and English, he was an obvious choice for Dvořák to take with him and his family to New York. He corresponded with Dvořák's biographer, Otakar Šourek, and his reminiscences are a valuable, though not always reliable, source of information about the composer's American stay: 'S Dvořákem v Americe' [With Dvořák in America], *Pestrá příloha Venkova* 9 (28 April and 5 May 1929); 'Dr. Ant. Dvořák, jak jsem ho znal' [Dr. Antonín Dvořák as I Knew Him], *Česká žena* 25 (29 April 1933), pp. 25–7; 'O Dvořákově komposiční škola v New Yorku' [About Dvořák's Composition Class in New York], *Podřipský kraj* 6 (1941), pp. 52–9; 'Dr. Dvořák as I Knew Him', *Fiddlestrings*, thirteen articles published between 1918 and 1928.

11 *Fiddlestrings* 3 (1920), pp. 3–4.
12 Waters, p. 86.

3 The Concerto and Dvořak's 'American manner'

1 Most influential of all commentators, Šourek introduced his discussion of the Concerto in his four-volume life-and-works by stating that the Concerto was not inspired by America, but arose from 'an immense artistic longing for Bohemia', Šourek 1956, p. 227. See also Chapter 6.

2 In his discussion of the *Te Deum* in *Antonín Dvořák: Musician and Craftsman* (London, 1966), pp. 259–60 [hereafter Clapham 1966], John Clapham notes a number of these proto-American traits. Michael Beckerman further explores the pastoral characteristics of Dvořák's American style in 'Dvořák's Pentatonic Landscape' in David Beveridge, ed., *Rethinking Dvořák: Views from Five Countries* (Oxford, 1996) [hereafter Beveridge 1996], pp. 245–54.

3 Gerald Abraham, in 'Dvořák's Musical Personality', in Viktor Fischl, ed., *Antonin Dvorak: His Achievement* (London, 1942) [hereafter Fischl], pp. 192–240, characterises this pentatonic colouring as 'the melodic "knight's move": the permutations and combinations of the first, fifth and sixth, or second, third and fifth degrees of the major scale' (Fischl, p. 205). To this might be added Dvořák's favourite variant: the third, fifth and sixth degrees of the scale.

4 For further information about the National Conservatory and Dvořák's role as Director see Emanuel Rubin, 'Dvořák at the National Conservatory', in John C. Tibbetts ed., *Dvořák in America, 1892–1895* (Portland, 1993) [hereafter Tibbetts], pp. 53–81, and Merton Robert Aborn, *The Influence on American Musical Culture of Dvořák's Sojourn in America*, Ph.D diss. (Ann Arbor, 1966).

5 Jeannette Thurber, 'Dvořák as I Knew Him', *The Etude* 37 (November 1919), pp. 693–4, reprinted in Tibbetts, pp. 380–2.

6 Though not entirely complete, many of the articles and interviews incorporating Dvořák's, often mediated, views are reprinted in Tibbetts Appendix A.

7 Reprinted in Michael Beckerman, ed., *Dvořák and His World* (Princeton, 1993) [hereafter Beckerman 1993], pp. 205–7.

8 Antonín Dvořák, 'For National Music', *Chicago Tribune* (13 August 1893); reprinted in Tibbetts pp. 361–2.

9 See Richard Crawford, 'Dvořák and the Historiography of American Music', and Charles Hamm, 'Dvořák, Nationalism, Myth, and Racism in the United States', in Beveridge 1996, pp. 257–64 and 275–80.

10 Printed in Beckerman 1993, pp. 204–5.

11 A. Dvořák in collaboration with Edwin Emerson Jr., 'Music in America', *Harper's New Monthly Magazine* (February 1895), reprinted in Tibbetts, pp. 370–80.

12 See Vojáčková-Wechte.

13 Unpublished letter dated 28 November 1890 from the estate of Mrs Burianová, copied by Josef Bartoš (among Bartoš' papers in the Museum of Czech Music).

14 Both letters are printed consecutively in Czech in Kuna 1989, pp. 184–90.

15 Clapham 1966, p. 103.

16 Antonín Dvořák, 'The Real Value of Negro Melodies', *New York Herald* (21 May 1893); most of the article is reprinted in Tibbetts, pp. 355–9. Some additional material missing from the reprint is to be found in M. Beckerman, 'The Real Value of Yellow Journalism: James Creelman and Antonín Dvořák', *The Musical Quarterly*, 77 (1993) pp. 749–68 (see esp. note 1) in which the author also speculates about James Creelman's role in the authorship of the article.

17 See Tibbetts, pp. 361–2.

18 The quote is taken from an unpublished letter from Kovařík to Dvořák's biographer Otakar Šourek from the estate of the late Jarmil Burghauser. Printed in Beckerman 1993, p. 141. The chapter in which the quote occurs, 'The Master's Little Joke: Antonín Dvořák and the Mask of Nation', is a fascinating consideration of the motives underlying Dvořák's American style by Michael Beckerman (pp. 134–54).

19 Clapham 1966, p. 105.

20 See Beveridge 1996, pp. 250–1.

21 Donald Francis Tovey, *Essays in Musical Analysis* III, *Concertos* (Oxford, 1936) [hereafter Tovey], p. 149.

22 In a letter to Alois Göbl, see Kuna 1989, pp. 328–31; see also Chapter 6.

4 'Decisions and revisions': sketch and compositional process

1 The various stages are laid out in Antonín Sychra, *Estetika Dvořákovy symfonické tvorby* [*The Aesthetic of Dvořák's Symphonic Compositions*] (Prague, 1959), pp. 389–90, partially reprinted in Clapham 1966, pp. 32–3.

2 See Burghauser and Šourek rev. edn of Antonín Dvořák, *Sinfonia IX*, Antonín Dvořák complete edition 111/9 (Prague, 1977), editors' notes; also Christian Rudolf Riedel, ed., Antonín Dvořák, *Symphonie No. 9* (Wiesbaden, 1995), preface.

3 See Burghauser, p. 317, and also complete edition 111/12, pp. 141–6.

4 For a fairly detailed description of the sketch, see Clapham 1979.

5 In the second bar of dominant preparation there is a diagonal line rising from left to right with a wavy line above it which might well be an indication of the chromatic scale for solo cello that leads into the recapitulation in the finished score. Interestingly, this passage of rising sixths and the final four quaver group before the sustained F-sharp may well have inspired the cello's last solo before the final tutti (bb. 338–41), also based on rising sixths.

6 See Clapham 1979, p. 126.

7 See the 'Select discography' for details. The removal of the extra passage in the coda would reduce Feuermann's performance from 10' 29" to 8' 28", and Rostropovich's from 13' 42" to 12' 54".

8 See Clapham 1979, p. 139.

5 The score I: forms and melodies

1 Alec Robertson, *Dvořák* (London, 1945) [hereafter Robertson], pp. 113–14.

2 *Ibid.*, p. 112.

3 *Ibid.*, p. 111.

4 Robertson, p. 114. The origins of this quote are somewhat obscure and we are indebted to Styra Avins for clarifying matters in *Johannes Brahms – Life and Letters* (Oxford, 1997) [hereafter Avins]. In note 5 on page 730 the author reveals that Florence May had the quote from Hausmann when preparing her two-volume life of Brahms. The quote as transmitted by May occurs in the following passage: 'He [Brahms] continued to take interest in important new compositions, and begged Hausmann to come to his rooms to play him Dvořák's Violoncello Concerto. He accompanied the entire work on the piano, and broke into enthusiastic admiration at the end of each movement, exclaiming after the last one, 'Had I known that such a violoncello Concerto as that could be written, I would have tried to compose one myself!' May, *The Life of Brahms* (London, 1905), vol. II, pp. 279–80. According to Avins,

Hausmann gave a similar quote to Tovey, see Tovey, p. 148. Avins is wrong, however, in assuming that Brahms proofread the concerto (see Avins, p. 729).

5 Chissell, 'The Symphonic Concerto', in Robert Layton, ed., *A Companion to the Concerto* (New York, 1989), pp. 152–76; the discussion of Dvořák's Concertos is on pp. 168–76.

6 Layton, *Dvořák Symphonies and Concertos* (London, 1978) [hereafter Layton 1978], p. 65.

7 'This movement [the first] is one of Dvořák's most inspired and best-constructed achievements in the symphonic field': Gervase Hughes, *Dvořák: His Life and Music* (London, 1967), p. 178; 'symphonically conceived with the solo instrument': Hans-Hubert Schönzeler, *Dvořák* (London, 1984)', p. 164; 'the first movement's brooding opening recalls Dvořák's monumental D minor Symphony (1884)': Robert Battey, 'Thoughts of Home: The Cello Concerto in B minor; Opus 104', in Tibbetts, p. 286.

8 David Beveridge, 'Romantic Ideas in a Classical Frame: the Sonata Forms of Dvořák', unpublished diss., University of California, Berkeley (1980), p. 392.

9 Letter to Brahms 28 December 1894, see Kuna 1989, pp. 339–42. Also partially quoted in Avins, p. 729.

10 Jiří Berkovec, *Antonín Dvořák* (Prague, 1969), p. 203.

11 Šourek 1956, p. 229. Šourek's extended treatment of the Concerto is found on pp. 227–38. An edited and reduced form in translation is to be found in Šourek, *The Orchestral Works of Antonín Dvořák*, trans. Roberta Finlayson-Samsour (Prague, 1956) [hereafter Šourek–Finlayson-Samsour], pp. 175–84. Knittl's comment in turn seems to echo the view of the critic of *The Musical Times* who reviewed the première on 19 March 1896; see note 14 below.

12 Karel Hoffmeister, *Antonín Dvořák* (Prague, 1924) [hereafter Hoffmeister]; the quotation is taken from Rosa Newmarch's serviceable, if slightly awkward, translation: *Antonín Dvořák* (London, 1928), p. 80.

13 *The Times* (20 March 1896).

14 *The Musical Times* 37 (1 April 1896), p. 239.

15 Interestingly, Casals 'cautioned against taking the second subject too slowly' (see David Blum, *Casals and the Art of Interpretation* (Berkeley, 1977) [hereafter Blum], p. 98). I will return to Casals' approach to the Concerto and his landmark recording in Chapter 7.

16 In his study of Brahms, to take but one example, Malcolm MacDonald characterises both of his Piano Concertos as 'symphonic'. See *Brahms* (London, 1990), pp. 99 and 275.

17 Hoffmeister, p. 80.

18 See Šourek 1956, p. 231 and Šourek–Finlayson-Samsour, p. 179.

19 Tovey, p. 150.

20 While Dvořák never whole-heartedly embraced Liszt's method of thematic metamorphosis, he approached it in his last symphonic poem, *The Hero's Song* (*Píseň Bohatýrská*, op. 111, B 199), composed two years after the Cello Concerto.

21 An exploration of what might be called Dvořák's 'Baroque tendencies' is to be found in Jan Smaczny, 'Dvořák and the Seconda Pratica', in Milan Pospíšil and Marta Ottlová, ed., *Antonín Dvořák 1841–1991* [Report of the International Musicological Congress, Dobříš, 1991] (Prague, 1994), pp. 271–80.

22 This is a good example of the way in which Dvořák, increasingly since the Eighth Symphony, exploited the rhythmic features of motifs in order to create links between otherwise disparate transitional elements.

23 Alan Houtchens, 'The F major String Quartet Opus 96', in Tibbetts, pp. 228–37.

24 See Arnold Schoenberg, 'New Music: My Music', in Leonard Stein, ed., and Leo Black, trans., *Style and Idea* (Berkeley, 1975), pp. 102–3.

25 *The Musical Times* (1 April 1896), p. 239.

26 *The Athenaeum* (28 March 1896), p. 421. This concert, which so enervated the critic of *The Athenaeum*, included Dvořák's Eighth Symphony, the première of his orchestration of the first five of his *Biblical Songs* (sung by Mrs Katherine Fisk), the Cello Concerto and a performance of Beethoven's 'Emperor' Concerto (Emil Sauer, piano, with the orchestra conducted by Sir Alexander Mackenzie).

27 *The Times* (20 March 1896).

28 With customary perceptiveness, Tovey appears to have been the first to have identified this transformation (see Tovey, p. 151); Šourek did not notice it at all.

29 See Clapham 1979, pp. 130–2.

30 The postal system between Prague and many places in Europe was extremely efficient. Letters and cards to England could take less than three days. The normal sailing time across the Atlantic (based on the Dvořáks' first trip to New York embarking at Bremen) could be as little nine days. In addition, a letter sent by Dvořák to his mother-in-law and children dated 7 December 1894 states that he had heard from Josefina; its contents seem to be a direct response to the letter of 26 November (see Kuna 1989, pp. 322–4, and Chapter 6).

31 See Michael Beckerman, 'Dvořák's "New World" Largo and the *Song of Hiawatha*', *19th Century Music*, 16 (1992), pp. 42–3.

32 In speaking about the fantasia-development of the finale, Clapham states: 'It is disappointing to see how Dvořák, the master of movement that he was, cobbles his bars together in the fantasia' (Clapham 1966, p. 92), and Tovey barely conceals his discomfort in a damagingly patronising analysis (Donald Tovey, *Symphonies and Other Orchestral Works* [reprint of *Essays in Musical Analysis*, first published 1935–9] (Oxford, 1989), pp. 288–9).

33 Tovey described the coda as a 'glorious series of epilogues in a steady progression of picturesqueness and calm' (Tovey, p. 152).

6 The score II: interpretations

1 See Burghauser, pp. 353 and 355; these unrealised projects were assigned the numbers B 418 and B 425, and occur in the second, third and fourth American sketchbooks respectively.

2 Burghauser, p. 351. It is possible that Dvořák was still pursuing thoughts along these lines when considering the G minor Concerto/Symphony (B 418) since there is a note relating to this material in the third American sketchbook detailing 'Corno', in a Lento movement, and 'Violi[no]', in a Largo movement.

3 *The Musical Times*, 37 (1 April 1896), p. 239. It is interesting to note how this comment not only echoes Knittl's view of the Concerto (see Chapter 5), but the reaction of the critic of *The Tribune* at the first performance of Herbert's Second Cello Concerto (see Chapter 2, n. 12).

4 *The Times* (20 March 1896).

5 Expressed crudely in terms of bar numbers, this amounts to the full tutti being deployed in thirty-five bars of the first movement, four of the second and forty-four of the third (a reasonable comparison would be with Dvořák's Violin Concerto where the tutti is involved in twenty-five bars of the first movement, twenty-five of the second and 108 of the finale).

6 Of course, the precedent for the quiet use of timpani had been well established, not least by Beethoven at the start of his Violin Concerto and end of his Fifth Piano Concerto; in the first movement of Brahms's First Piano Concerto there is a gentle underpinning of the first entry of the piano, and a drum roll provides the background for the entry of the violin in the first movement of his Violin Concerto.

7 The use of this figure seems to have been prompted by Wihan; see Chapter 7.

8 Percy M. Young, *Elgar OM, A Study of a Musician* (London, 1955), p. 56. For an extended consideration of Dvořák's impact on Elgar see Graham Melville-Mason, 'Dvořák and Elgar', in Beveridge 1996, pp. 225–33.

9 See Šourek–Finlayson-Samsour, p. 184.

10 Robertson, p. 114.

11 See Tibbetts, p. 290.

12 Michael Beckerman, 'Dvořák's "New World" Largo and *The Song of Hiawatha*', *19th Century Music*, 16 (1992), pp. 35–48.

13 Undated letter from Kovařík to Šourek in Beckerman, *ibid.*, pp. 36–7 (Beckerman's translation). The author is grateful to Professor Beckerman for allowing the use of his translation.

14 *The Musical Times*, 38 (1 September 1897), p. 620.

15 These included an extensive revision of *The Jacobin* (op. 84, B 200), *The Devil and Kate* (*Čert a Káča*, op. 112, B 201), *Rusalka* (op. 114, B 202) and *Armida* (op. 115, B 206).

16 See Bedřich Smetana, *Libuše* [vocal score] (Prague, 1956), pp. 143–53.

17 Edwin Evans, 'The Symphonies and Concertos', in Fischl, p. 93.

18 Šourek 1956, p. 227.

19 Šourek–Finlayson-Samsour, p. 175. In fact, this quote predates Šourek 1956 since Šourek–Finlayson-Samsour is a translation of Šourek's volume on the orchestral music published in 1946 (*Dvořákovy skladby orchestrální II* (Prague, 1946).

20 Robert Battey, 'Thoughts of Home: The Cello Concerto in B Minor, Opus 104', in Tibbetts, pp. 284–93.

21 Letter to Göbl of 10 December 1894; printed in Czech in Kuna 1989, pp. 328–31.

22 Letter to Boleška of 15 January 1895, printed in Czech in Kuna 1989, pp. 363–5.

23 Otakar Šourek, *Život a dílo Antonína Dvořáka* [*Life and Works of Antonín Dvořák*], 3rd edn, vol. I (Prague, 1954), pp. 75 ff. Šourek's information probably came from members of Dvořák's family, with whom he had extensive dealings in his work on the composer, and has been accepted as true by all authorities, including all subsequent editors of the Dvořák complete edition.

24 Otakar Dvořák, *Antonín Dvořák, My Father*, ed. Paul J. Polansky, and trans. Miroslav Němec (Spillville, 1993), p. 59. This problematic source needs careful handling and is full of errors, including the statement that Dvořák was prompted by the playing of Stern in America (!) to compose the Cello Concerto and the citing of a non-existent première of the Cello Concerto also in America (see p. 55).

25 See Šourek, *Život a dílo Antonína Dvořáka*, vol. I, p. 75.

26 For a list of the various uses Dvořák made of the cycle see Jan Smaczny, 'Dvořák's "Cypresses": A Song Cycle and its Metamorphoses', *Music & Letters* 71 (1991), pp. 552–68; reprinted in Beveridge 1996, pp. 55–70.

27 For a full translation see Clapham 1979, pp. 131–2.

28 This included the 'New World' Symphony.

29 Clapham 1979, p. 132. This article includes a translation of the letter.

30 See Kuna 1989, pp. 322–4. See also n. 30 in Chapter 5.

31 See Kuna 1989, pp. 331–2. In another letter of 11 January 1895 Dvořák stated that he would write to Josefina ('Pepi') at once; see Kuna 1989, pp. 356–9.

32 See Šourek–Finlayson-Samsour, p. 176; see also the introduction to the songs in the Dvořák complete edition (VI/2, 1957) in which František Bartoš, using information from Šourek, states that the song was dear to her.

33 'Lasst mich allein! Verscheucht den Frieden nicht in meiner Brust mit euren lauten Worten'. Dvořák took the poems from a collection by Ottilie Maly-brock-Stieler (1836–1913) entitled *Lyrische Gedichte und Übertragungen nach böhmischer Kunst- und Volkspoesie* published in 1887. He originally set them in German; V. J. Novotný later wrote in his Czech translation which is the version published in the complete edition (see Burghauser, pp. 269–71).

34 See Šourek 1956, p. 290.

35 Tovey, p. 148.

36 Jitka Slavíková, 'A Brief Observation on the Finale of the Cello Concerto', in Milan Pospíšil and Marta Ottlová, eds., *Antonín Dvořák 1841–1991* (Prague, 1994), pp. 293–5.

37 Dvořák wrote to Tchaikovsky referring to the opera as a 'wonderful piece, full of burning emotion and poetry' (see the letter to Tchaikovsky in Milan Kuna, ed., *Antonín Dvořák: korespondence a dokumenty*, vol. II (Prague, 1988), pp. 359–61).

38 Clapham 1966, p. 234.

39 My translation. For a line-by-line translation, see Beveridge 1996, p. 42.

40 See Blum, p. 4.

41 Letter to Simrock. See Kuna 1989, pp. 422–4.

42 The sustained struggle by Zdeněk Nejedlý to diminish Dvořák's reputation accounted for some devastatingly destructive criticism of the composer's work in the twentieth century. Dvořák was frequently depicted by Nejedlý and his followers as a naïve, unreflective, eclectic conservative whose works stood in opposition to the progressive tendencies of Smetana. The dynamics of this discreditable episode in the history of Czech musicology are admirably charted in Marta Ottlová's chapter 'The "Dvořák Battles" in Bohemia', in Beveridge 1996, pp. 126–33.

7 Performers and performances

1 For an account of this relationship see Willi Schuh, *Richard Strauss: A Chronicle of the Early Years 1864–1898*, trans. Mary Whittall (Cambridge, 1982), pp. 161–74.

2 See Kuna 1989, pp. 370–3.

3 Some details of Wihan's suggestions are given in the critical notes to the complete edition score (ed. Šourek (Prague, 1955), pp. 147–60; English commentary, pp. 143–4).

4 Dvořák had given a musical illustration of the wind, solo cello and viola parts at the start of this passage in the letter to Göbl of 10 December 1894 which had detailed his feelings about the second subject of the first movement (see Kuna 1989, pp. 328–31). Although the figure for the solo cello starts with the lower note (as opposed to the higher, as in his later versions), it is clear that from the start he intended a semiquaver oscillation.

5 This recording with George Szell and the Czech Philharmonic Orchestra is available in no fewer than six separate CD issues (see the Select Discography).

6 Casals leaves the pizzicato notes out in bar 117 rather than attempting an alternation of chord and pizzicato favoured by some performers.

7 *The Musical Times*, 37 (1 April 1896), p. 239.

8 Now in the Dvořák Museum in Prague.

9 These disputed passages were printed with 'ossias' (Movement 1: bars 261–5; 327–30; 334–5; 338–40. Movement 3: bars 187–8; 199–202). See Simrock 1896, and Complete Edition Score, 1955.

10 See Kuna 1989, pp. 422–4. Despite the lofty tone of the letter, Dvořák concluded it in a more practical mood by suggesting a fee of 6,000 marks for the Concerto and *Te Deum* together.

11 Milan Kuna, ed., *Antonín Dvořák korespondence a dokumenty* [*Antonín Dvořák: Correspondence and Documents*], vol. IV: *1896–1904* (Prague, 1995), pp. 14–15 [hereafter Kuna 1995].

12 See *ibid*, p. 15.

13 See *ibid*, pp. 16–17.

14 See *ibid*, pp. 17–19.

15 *The Times* (20 March 1896).

16 See Margaret Campbell, *The Great Cellists* (London, 1988) [hereafter Campbell], p. 127.

17 *The Musical Times*, 37 (April 1896), p. 239.

18 See Campbell, p. 127.

19 *The Athenaeum* (28 March 1896), p. 421.

20 18 March 1896; see Kuna 1995, p. 22.

21 10 April 1896; see Kuna 1995, pp. 25–6.

22 Most details regarding early performances of the Concerto are derived from Burghauser 1996, pp. 715–17 and 738.

23 Robertson, p. 116.

24 See review printed in Robert Baldock, *Pablo Casals* (London, 1992), p. 270, n. 27.

25 See *ibid*, pp. 124–5.

26 See *ibid*, p. 153.

27 See Blum, pp. 86–7. Although most soloists pull back at this point, including Feuermann, in fact the *ritardando* mark is seven bars into the passage. Casals is punctilious in following his own advice.

28 See Blum, p. 98.

29 Aspects of the orchestration also seem to underpin a prevailing desire to preserve a sense of motion; in the A-flat minor section of the development of the first movement the pizzicato notes in the string bass give added impetus to the down beats from bar 5 (see Ex. 5.1).

30 In an additional note to Robert Battey's chapter on the Concerto in Tibbetts (see p. 292) the editor includes an excerpt from an interview with the cellist Lynn Harrell, who speaks expressively of just these features of the work.

Select bibliography

Abraham, Gerald. 'Dvořák's Musical Personality', in Fischl, ed., *Antonin Dvorak: His Achievement*, 192–240; re-edited in Abraham, *Slavonic and Romantic Music* (London, 1968), 40–69

Avins, Styra (translated, with Josef Eisinger, and annotated). *Johannes Brahms: Life and Letters* (Oxford, 1997)

Baldock, Robert. *Pablo Casals* (London, 1992)

Battey, Robert. 'Thoughts of Home: The Cello Concerto in B minor, Opus 104', in Tibbetts, ed., *Dvořák in America, 1892–1895*, 284–93

Beckerman, Michael. 'Dvořák's "New World" Largo and *The Song of Hiawatha*', *19th Century Music* 16 (Summer 1992), 35–48

'The Real Value of Yellow Journalism: James Creelman and Antonín Dvořák', *The Musical Quarterly* 77 (1993), 749–68

'The Master's Little Joke: Antonín Dvořák and the Mask of Nation', in Beckerman, ed., *Dvořák and His World*, 134–54

'Dvořák's Pentatonic Landscape', in Beveridge, ed., *Rethinking Dvořák: Views from Five Countries*, 245–54

Beckerman, Michael, ed., *Dvořák and His World* (Princeton, 1993)

Berkovec, Jiří. *Antonín Dvořák* (Prague, 1969)

Beveridge, David. 'Romantic Ideas in a Classical Frame: The Sonata Forms of Dvořák' (Ph.D. diss., University of California, Berkeley (1980); Diss. Abstracts 42:11A. Ann Arbor: University Microfilms International, 1981)

Beveridge, David, ed., *Rethinking Dvořák: Views from Five Countries* (Oxford, 1996)

Blum, David. *Casals and the Art of Interpretation* (Berkeley, 1977)

Broadly, Arthur. *Chats to Cello Students* (London, 1899)

The Violoncello: Its History, Selection and Adjustment (London, 1921)

Burghauser, Jarmil. *Antonín Dvořák: thematický katalog* [*Antonín Dvořák: Thematic Catalogue*] (Prague, 1996)

Campbell, Margaret. *The Great Cellists* (London, 1988)

Chissell, Joan. 'The Concerto after Beethoven: (ii) The Symphonic Concerto', in Layton, ed., *A Companion to the Concerto*, 152–76

Clapham, John. ''Dvořák's First Cello Concerto', *Music & Letters* 37 (1956), 350–5

   Antonín Dvořák: Musician and Craftsman (London, 1966)

   Dvořák (London, 1979)

   'Dvořák's Cello Concerto in B minor: A Masterpiece in the Making', *Music Review* 40 (1979), 123–40

Crawford, Richard. 'Dvořák and the Historiography of American Music', in Beveridge, ed., *Rethinking Dvořák: Views from Five Countries* , 257–64.

Dvořák, Antonín. 'For National Music, Dvořák, the Great Bohemian Artist, Explains his Ideas', *Chicago Tribune* (12 August 1893), in Tibbetts, ed., *Dvořák in America, 1892–1895*, 361–2

   'The Real Value of Negro Melodies', *New York Herald* (21 May 1893), in Tibbetts, ed., *Dvořák in America, 1892–1895*, 355–9

Dvořák, Antonín, in collaboration with Edwin Emerson Jr., 'Music in America', *Harper's New Monthly Magazine*, 48 (1894), 341–6, in Tibbetts, ed., *Dvořák in America, 1892–1895*, 370–80

Dvořák, Otakar. *Antonín Dvořák, My Father* [edited by Paul J. Polansky and translated by Miroslav Němec] (Spillville, 1993)

Evans, Edwin, 'The Symphonies and Concertos', in Fischl, ed., *Antonin Dvorak: His Achievement*, 71–95

Fischl, Viktor. *Antonin Dvorak: His Achievement* (London, 1942)

Hamm, Charles. 'Dvořák, Nationalism, Myth, and Racism in the United States', in Beveridge, ed., *Rethinking Dvořák: Views from Five Countries*, 275–80

Hill, Ralph, ed., *The Concerto* (London, 1952)

Hoffmeister, Karel. *Antonín Dvořák* (Prague, 1924), translated by Rosa Newmarch as *Antonín Dvořák* (London, 1928)

Hopkins, Antony. *Talking about Concertos* (London, 1970)

Hughes, Gervase. *Dvořák: His Life and Music* (London, 1967)

Kovařík, Joseph Jan. 'S Dvořákem v Americe' ['With Dvořák in America'], *Pestrá příloha Venkova* (28 April and 5 May 1929)

   'Dr. Ant. Dvořák, jak jsem ho znál' ['Dr. Antonín Dvořák as I Knew Him'], *Česká žena* (St. Louis, Mo.) 25 (29 April 1933), 25–7

   'O Dvořákově komposiční škola v New Yorku' ['About Dvořák's Composition Class in New York'], *Podřipský kraj* 6 (1941), 52–9

   'Dr. Dvořák as I Knew Him', *Fiddlestrings*: thirteen articles published between 1918 and 1928

Kuna, Milan, ed., *Antonín Dvořák: korespondence a dokumenty* [*Antonín Dvořák: Correspondence and Documents*], vol. III: *1890–1895* (Prague, 1989); vol. IV: *1896–1904* (Prague, 1995)

Layton, Robert. *Dvořák Symphonies and Concertos* (London, 1978)

Layton, Robert, ed., *A Companion to the Concerto* (New York, 1989)

Marx, Klaus with Malcolm Boyd and Sonya Monosoff. 'The Violoncello', in Sadie, ed., *The Violin Family* [The New Grove Dictionary of Musical Instruments Series] (London, 1989), 153–82

May, Florence. *The Life of Brahms*, 2 vols. (London, 1905)

Melville-Mason, Graham. 'Dvořák and Elgar', in Beveridge, ed., *Rethinking Dvořák: Views from Five Countries*, 225–33

Michl, Joseph. 'Z Dvořákova vyprávění' ['From the Dvořák Narrative'], *Hudební revue*, 7 (1914), 400–4, 440–6

Ottlová, Marta. 'The "Dvořák Battles" in Bohemia', in Beveridge, ed., *Rethinking Dvořák: Views from Five Countries*, 126–33

Pospíšil, Milan and Marta Ottlová, eds., *Antonín Dvořák, Report of the International Musicological Congress, Dobříš, 1991* (Prague, 1994)

Robertson, Alec. *Dvořák* (London, 1945)

Rubin, Emanuel. 'Dvořák at the National Conservatory', in Tibbetts, ed., *Dvořák in America, 1892–1895*, 53–81

Salter, Lionel. 'Antonín Dvořák (1841–1904)', in Hill, ed., *The Concerto*, 234–45

Schönzeler, Hans-Hubert. *Dvořák* (London, 1984)

Slavíková, Jitka. 'A Brief Observation on the Finale of the Cello Concerto', in Pospíšil and Ottlová (eds.), *Antonín Dvořák: Report of the International Musicological Congress, Dobříš, 1991*, 293–5

Smaczny, Jan. '*Alfred*: Dvořák's First Operatic Endeavour Surveyed', *Journal of the Royal Musical Association* 115 (1990), 80–106

'Dvořák's "Cypresses": A Song Cycle and its Metamorphoses', *Music & Letters* 72 (1991), 552–68

'Dvořák and the Seconda Pratica', in Pospíšil and Ottlová, eds., *Antonín Dvořák, Report of the International Musicological Congress, Dobříš 1991*, 271–80

'The Czech Symphony', in Layton, ed., *A Companion to the Symphony* (reprint Oxford, 1995), 221–61

Šourek, Otakar. 'Wihanova kadence k Dvořákovu koncertu' ['Wihan's Cadenza to Dvořák's Concerto'], *Hudební výchova* 17 (1936), 109–10

Život a dílo Antonína Dvořáka [*The Life and Works of Antonín Dvořák*], vol. I: *1841–1877*, third edn (Prague, 1954)

Život a dílo Antonína Dvořáka [*The Life and Works of Antonín Dvořák*], vol. III: *1891–1896*, second edn (Prague, 1956)

The Orchestral Works of Antonín Dvořák, trans. Roberta Finlayson-Samsour (Prague, 1956)

Straeten, Edmund S. J. van der. *History of the Violoncello, the Viol da Gamba, their Precursors and Collateral Instruments with Biographies of the Most Eminent Players of Every Country* (London, 1914; reprinted 1971)

Sychra, Antonín. *Estetika Dvořákovy symfonické tvorby* [*The Aesthetic of Dvořák's Symphonic Composition*] (Prague, 1959)

Thurber, Jeannette. 'Dvořák as I Knew Him', *The Etude* 37 (November 1919), in Tibbetts, ed., *Dvořák in America, 1892–1895*, 693–4

Tibbetts, John C., ed., *Dvořák in America, 1892–1895* (Portland, 1993)

Tovey, Donald Francis. *Essays in Musical Analysis*, vol. III: *Concertos* (London, 1936)

Urie, Bedřich. *Čeští violoncellisté* [*Czech Cellists*] (Prague, 1949)

Vojačková-Wechte, Ludmila. 'Antonín Dvořák in the Class Room', *The Etude* 37 (March 1919), 135

Wasielewski, Wilhelm Joseph von. *The Violoncello and Its History*, trans. Isobella S. E. Stigand (London, 1894)

Waters, Edward N. *Victor Herbert: A Life in Music* (New York, 1955)

Whitehouse, William Edward. *Recollections of a Violoncellist* (London, 1930)

Select discography

The following list includes, in chronological order of recording, the performances referred to in the text.

Emanuel Feuermann with the Berlin State Opera House Orchestra, cond. Michael Taube: *The Young Feuermann* – Pearl: Gemm CD 9077 (1928/29)

Pablo Casals with the Czech Philharmonic Orchestra, cond. Georg Szell – Dutton: Essential Archive (the HMV recordings), CDEA5002 (1937)*

Emanuel Feuermann with the National Orchestral Association, cond. Leon Barzin – Philips: Legendary Classics, Philips 420 776–2 (1940)

Maurice Gendron with the Paris Radio Orchestra, cond. Willem Mengelberg: *The Mengelberg Edition* Vol. 10 – Archive Documents ABCD 116 (1944)

André Navarra with the Prague Radio Symphony Orchestra, cond. František Stupka: *Prague Spring Collection* – Multisonic 31 0039–2 (1951)

Pierre Fournier with the Berlin Philharmonic Orchestra, cond. George Szell – Deutsche Grammophon: Galleria 423 881–2 (1962)

Mstislav Rostropovich with the Berlin Philharmonic Orchestra, cond. Herbert von Karajan – Deutsche Grammophon: Legendary Recordings from the Deutsche Grammophon Catalogue 447 413–2 (1968)

Mstislav Rostropovich with the London Philharmonic Orchestra, cond. Carlo Maria Giulini – EMI CDC 7 49306 2 (1977)

Paul Tortelier with the London Symphony Orchestra, cond. André Previn – EMI: Studio CDM 7 69169 2 (1977)

Lynn Harrell with the Philharmonia Orchestra, cond. Vladimir Ashkenazy – Decca 410 144–2 (1982)

Maria Kliegel with the Royal Philharmonic Orchestra, cond. Michael Halász – Naxos 8.550503 (1991)

Yo-Yo Ma with the New York Philharmonic Orchestra, cond. Kurt Masur – Sony Classical: SK 67 173 (1995)

* Casals' 1937 recording is available on a number of labels: EMI CDH7 63496–2; MSCM MM30426; PEAR GEMMCDS9935; PEAR GEMMCD9349; MAGT CD48023

Index

Abraham, Gerald, 101 n. 3
Albani, Emma, 91
Ashkenazy, Vladimir, 97

Banner, Michael, 22
Bartók, Béla, 64
Bartoš, František, 108 n. 32
Bartoš, Josef, 102 n. 13
Battey, Robert, 71
Becker, Hugo, 93
Beckerman, Michael, 27, 58, 71, 101 n.
    2, 102 nn. 16 and 18, 107 n. 13
Beethoven, Ludwig van, 1, 29, 42, 105
    n. 26, 106 n. 6
Berger, Francesco, 91
Berkovec, Jiří, 43
Beveridge, David, 43
Blum, David, 84
Boleška, Josef, 76, 77
Brahms, Johannes, 42, 43, 46, 68, 103–4
    n. 4, 104 n. 16, 106 n. 6
Buck, Percy, 70
Burghauser, Jarmil, 99 n. 10, 100 n. 5,
    102 n. 18
Burleigh, Harry Thacker, 22

Carnegie, Andrew, 22
Casals, Pablo, 84, 87, **93–7**, 98, 104 n. 15,
    109 n. 6, 110 n. 27
Cello Concerto
    cello solo in relation to the orchestra,
        11–19 (*passim*), 64–71, 89, 110
        n. 29
    compared to first Cello Concerto,
        3–7

contemporary critics, 43–4, 54, 57, 58,
    62, 64–5, 89, 91–2, 104 n. 11, 105
    n. 26, 106 n. 3
Dvořák's 'American' style and the
    concerto, 14, **20–8**, 42, 43, 57
Dvořák's attitude to cello, **1–2**, **7–10**,
    11–19, 86
Josefina and the concerto, ix, 28, 31,
    37, 40, 41, **77–85**, 90, 98, 101 n. 1
metronome markings, 44, 94, 96, 97
nostalgia, 24, **75–7**
objections to cadenza, 18, **89–90**
operatic and lyrical qualities, 44, **71–5**
première(s), 89, **90–3**, 107 n. 24, 109
    n. 22
sketches, 13–14, **29–41**, 49, 61, 62, 100
    nn. 5 and 6, 103 n. 5
solo cello figuration, 4, 5–6, 12, 18, 26,
    35, 52, 68, 69, 70, 87, 88, 89, 90,
    106 n. 7
symphonic characteristics, **42–6**, 54,
    72
first movement, 2, 3–4 (*passim*), 5, 6,
    7, 17, 18–19, 25, 26, 27, 28, 29,
    32–5, 36, 37, 40, 42, 43, 44, 45,
    46–54, 58, 60, 61, 62, 63, 64, 65, 66,
    67, 68, 72, 73, 74, 76, 77, 82, 84, 87,
    88, 89, 94, 95, 96 (Table 7.2), 97, 103
    n. 5, 106 n. 5, 109 n. 4, 110 n. 29
recapitulation, 6, 18–19, 34, 47, 48
    (Ex. 5.2), 49, 52, 58, 77, 96, 97, 98,
    103 n. 5
second theme, 27, 32, 33 (Ex. 4.2b),
    34, 44, 47–9, 52, 65, 73–4, 76, 77,
    95–6, 109 n. 4

116

Index